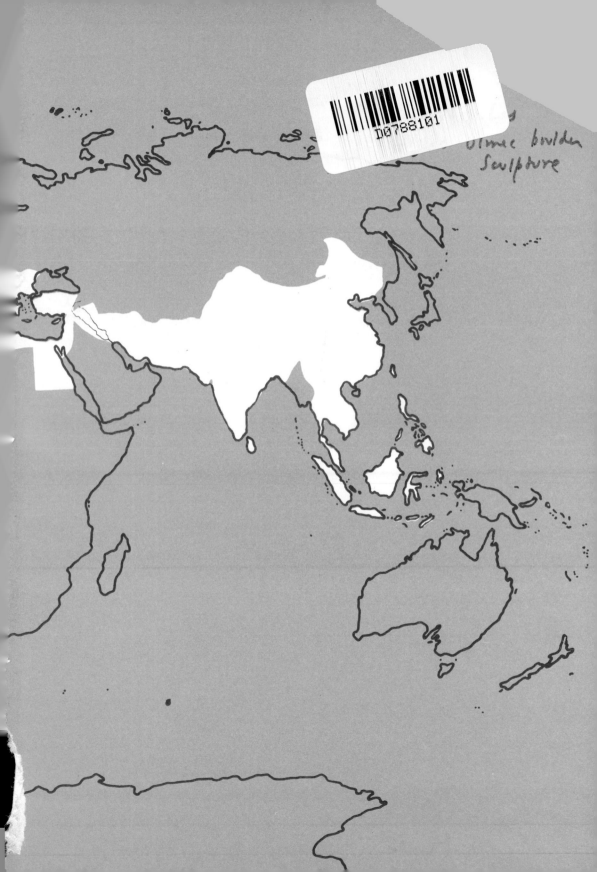

olmec boulder
Sculpture

INDONESIA	Bernard P. Groslier, Curator of Historical Monuments, Angkor; Director of Archaeological Research at the Ecole Française d'Extrême-Orient
JAPAN	Vadime Elisseeff, Curator at the Cernuschi Museum, Paris
MESOPOTAMIA	Jean-Claude Margueron, Agrégé of the University, Paris; Member of the French Institute of Archaeology of Beirut
MEXICO	Jacques Soustelle
PERSIA I (From the origins to the Achaemenids)	Jean-Louis Huot, Agrégé of the University, Paris; Member of the French Institute of Archaeology of Beirut
PERSIA II (From the Seleucids to the Sassanids)	Vladimir Lukonin, Head of the Oriental Department, Hermitage Museum, Leningrad
PERU	† Rafael Larco Hoyle, Director of the Rafael Larco Herrera Museum, Lima
PREHISTORY	Denise de Sonneville-Bordes, Ph. D.
ROME	Gilbert Picard, Professor at the Sorbonne, Paris
RUMANIA	Constantin Daicoviciu, Director of the Archaeological Institute of Cluj, and Emil Condurachi, Director of the Archaeological Institute of Bucarest
SOUTHERN CAUCASUS	Boris B. Piotrovsky, Director of the Hermitage Museum, Leningrad
SOUTHERN SIBERIA	Mikhail Gryaznov, Professor at the Archaeological Institute, Leningrad
SYRIA-PALESTINE I (Ancient Orient)	Jean Perrot, Head of the French Archaeological Mission in Israel
SYRIA-PALESTINE II (Classical Orient)	Michael Avi Yonah, Professor at the University of Jerusalem
THE TEUTONS	R. Hachmann, Professor at the University of Saarbrücken
TIBET	Giuseppe Tucci, President of the Italian Institute for the Middle and Far East, Rome
URARTU	Boris B. Piotrovsky, Director of the Hermitage Museum, Leningrad

ARCHAEOLOGIA MVNDI

Series prepared under the direction of Jean Marcadé,
Professor of Archaeology at the University of Bordeaux

CLAUDE F. BAUDEZ

CENTRAL AMERICA

Translated from the French by James Hogarth

54 illustrations in colour; 106 illustrations in black and white

NAGEL PUBLISHERS, GENEVA · PARIS · MUNICH

CONTENTS

PREFACE

*I*t is the purpose of the Archaeologia Mundi *series to bring out the varying aspects of archaeology in the different parts of the world with which it is concerned. For of course the problems, the methods and the results of archaeology vary according to the natural setting and historical background of the different countries, and also according to the practical conditions in which archaeological research has to be carried out.*

In certain areas archaeology has long been active. In others its development has been much more recent—either because the attention of scholars has been concentrated on some great neighbouring civilisation or because the remains of the past have been so scanty or so difficult to distinguish that they have for long escaped systematic observation and reasoned analysis.

We can see these factors at work in Central America, in the sense in which the term is used in this book. Honduras, El Salvador, Nicaragua, Costa Rica and Panama, lying under the shadow of the great civilisations of Yucatán and Mexico, have hitherto had little attention from archaeologists. The lack of any real epigraphic material and the meagre remains of occupied sites have been further obstacles to the study of the pre-Columbian past of these regions.

The special interest of M. Baudez' book is that it illustrates, in the circumstances of this particular area, the difficulties of archaeological study in an almost unexplored field, sets out the principles on which this study should be based, and summarises the provisional conclusions which can be drawn on the basis of the evidence so far available.

J. M.

This book could not have been produced without the ready help and cooperation which the author has received from a large number of people. To all of them he would like to express his sincere thanks:

— in the first place to Mr Jack Birchall, who took almost all the photographs;
— in El Salvador, to Dr M. A. Fogoaga, Director of the Museo Nacional, to Sres Walter Soundy and Tomás de Vilanova, and to Sra Dolly de Mena Ariz;
— in Honduras, to Sr Vinelli, Director of the Banco Atlántida, and to Sras Agurcia and Sempé;
— in Nicaragua, to Professor Gregorio Aguilar, Director of the Juigalpa Museum, and to Sres Enrique Neret and Mario Belli of Managua;
— in Costa Rica, to Professor Carlos Melendez, of the University of Costa Rica, for his enthusiastic encouragement; and to Sr Hector Gamboa of the Museo Nacional, Sras Oduber and Goicoechea, Sr Juan Dada, and others who kindly made their collections available to the author;
— in Panama, to Sra Reina Torres de Araúz, Professor of Anthropology at the University of Panama, who was always ready with counsel and support; and to Dr Alejandro Méndez, Director of the Museo Nacional, and Sres Canavaggio, Ferrari and Trujillo.

Finally the author would like to express his gratitude to his colleagues Mme Simoni and M. Ichon for their help in identifying certain items, and particularly to M. Becquelin, who kindly read the manuscript and contributed greatly towards its improvement with his criticisms and suggestions.

C.F. B.

INTRODUCTION

I

The Natural Setting

Anarrow bridge joining two sub-continents, an area of transition and exchange between North and South, an area of passage and a meeting place not only for men but for plants and animals: these are the characteristics which make the Central American isthmus a complex and fascinating object of study for the naturalist and the anthropologist alike.

For the purposes of this survey Central America is defined as the part of the isthmus between Guatemala in the west and Colombia in the east. Five states—Honduras, El Salvador, Nicaragua, Costa Rica and Panama— share a territory which is of relatively limited extent (some 157,000 square miles, compared with 89,000 for Great Britain and 210,000 for France) but stretches from the 7th to the 16th degree of northern latitude[1].

The geographical pattern of the isthmus can conveniently be described in three zones of unequal width. These are, from west to east, the Pacific zone, the central highland zone and the Caribbean zone.

The Pacific Zone

The backbone of the isthmus is a volcanic chain of recent origin which runs from north-west to south-east throughout its entire length from the Mexico-Guatemala frontier to central Costa Rica—a total distance of over 900 miles. Under the influence of the prevailing north-easterly winds (the trade winds) the fertile volcanic ashes were—and still are—deposited to the west and south of the chain, where they renewed themselves and fructified—a bounty which was denied to central Honduras and northern Nicaragua.

I

Two large lakes, Managua and Nicaragua, covering an area 100 miles long by 45 miles across, occupy the great Nicaraguan depression which extends from the mouth of the San Juan river on the Caribbean coast to the Gulf of Fonseca on the Pacific.

The Central Valley of Costa Rica, lying between the southern tip of the central volcanic chain and a group of hills of Tertiary date, comprises the basins of San José and Cartago, to whose fertile soil a number of volcanoes have contributed. Farther south the isthmus is almost entirely occupied by the cordillera of Talamanca, which is followed by a series of volcanic chains, mainly of Tertiary date, extending throughout Panama as far as the Canal Zone. Beyond these again are the mountains of Darien, a continuation of the cordillera of the Andes, with an alternation of volcanic and sedimentary rocks. In the highlands of Costa Rica and western Panama the year is divided into two seasons, a wet one *(invierno)* and a dry one *(verano)*, the latter beginning in mid December and lasting until April. The annual rainfall ranges between 2000 and 3500 mm.

A narrow coastal strip runs in a straight line along the Pacific coast of El Salvador and Nicaragua, interrupted only by the Gulf of Fonseca. Beyond this to the south is the irregular and tormented coastline of Costa Rica and Panama. The coastal plain is of some width until the Gulf of Panama, and the province of Coclé occupies a depression between the Central Cordillera and the Azuero peninsula. Throughout this area the two seasons are clearly distinguished from one another and share the year equally between them, with a total rainfall ranging from 1000 to 2000 mm. The long and practically rainless *verano* is responsible for the predominance of deciduous trees. Variations from this pattern are found in the Golfo Dulce area (south-western Costa Rica) and the Azuero peninsula (Panama), which have an annual rainfall of up to 4000 mm. and are covered with tropical forest.

The Highlands of Honduras and Northern Nicaragua

This is the part of Central America where the rocks are most folded. Mountain chains with a broad east-west orientation and composed mainly of ancient metamorphic rocks have been covered in central Honduras and northern Nicaragua with thick volcanic deposits of Tertiary date. On the north coast of Honduras a series of tectonic basins or depressions oriented from north-east to south-west open into the Caribbean, traversed by a number of rivers (the Chamelecón, the Ulúa, the Aguán, etc.) which enrich them with deposits of fertile alluvium. Elsewhere in the highlands the only areas of flat ground are a number of mountain basins, the "valleys" of Comayagua, Otoro and Sensenti. The rainy season, from May to November, is interrupted by the *veranillo*, a period of from two to five weeks in July or August during which the rain stops. The total annual rainfall varies from 1000 to 2000 mm. The mountains, with a meagre covering of soil, are clad to a height of 2000 metres with forests of oak and pine, with a marked predominance of the latter.

The Caribbean Coast

The Mosquitia is a large coastal plain occupying eastern Nicaragua and much of north-eastern Honduras and consisting mainly of gravels and sandy clays of marine origin. The alluvial soil deposited by the San Juan, which drains Lake Nicaragua, has played a considerable part in the building up of the Caribbean coast of Costa Rica in recent times. The plain comes to an end at the frontier of Panama, whose northern coast is much indented, with volcanic hills extending right down to the coast. Exposed as it is to the trade winds, the Caribbean coast is the wettest part of Central America, with an average annual rainfall of over 2000 mm. and a recorded peak of 5000 mm. In this region the *verano* (February-March) and the *veranillo* (July-August) cannot be called dry seasons: at best they can be described as being less wet than the rest of the year. Apart from the

Mosquitia plain, an area of savanna with a sprinkling of pines, this is a region of humid tropical forest.

Fauna

From the zoological point of view Central America is the meeting place of a variety of species of different origins; the fauna is predominantly South American, with an admixture of North American species. To mention only the species of importance to man, there are deer (a North American and a South American species), peccaries, the tapir, the agouti, and smaller species like monkeys, coatis, armadillos, rabbits, sloths, etc. Among birds hunted either for their flesh or their plumage are the tinamou, the curassow, the chachalaca and others more familiar to us—turkeys, migrant ducks, parrots and parrakeets, humming-birds and the famous quetzal. The chief predators are the large felines of South America (the jaguar, the ocelot, the margay and the jaguarundi) and the North American puma. The reptiles mostly play a negative part (crocodiles, poisonous snakes), but may sometimes be hunted as game (large lizards, iguanas). The resources of the sea include, in addition to fish and shellfish, the large turtles and their eggs.

Environments and Resources

In general the highlands of Honduras and northern Nicaragua do not lend themselves to the establishment of settled human groups. The rugged contours and the general poverty of the soil impose severe limitations on the development of agriculture. The well watered basins of fertile alluvial soil which cut through the mountains along the northern coast of Honduras do, however, offer favourable conditions for farming. The mountain basins of the interior occupy an intermediate position, varying according to their particular resources, between the poverty of the mountains and the wealth of the coastal valleys.

The Caribbean side of Honduras and Nicaragua comprises an area of tropical forest and the savanna land of the Mosquitia. In both areas the soil (gravel and sand) is poor, and the inhabitants have had to establish themselves on the alluvial soil brought down by the rivers or to exploit the resources of the coastal lagoons.

The relative wealth of most of the Pacific coast has already been noted. The most favourable conditions are to be found in El Salvador, where there are active volcanoes which frequently renew the soil with their deposits of ash. This is the region with the highest population density in the whole of Central America. The soil of the Nicoya peninsula (Costa Rica), although of different origin, is sufficiently fertile to yield crops for anything from six to ten successive years. Another area favourable to agriculture is the Central Valley of Costa Rica, which contains the bulk of the country's population. In Panama the area with the greatest possibilities is perhaps the savanna region which extends as far as the Canal between the Central Cordillera, clad with tropical forests, to the north and the Azuero peninsula to the south. To the east of the Canal is the jungle-covered province of Darien, forming the extreme southern tip of the isthmus.

On both the Caribbean and the Pacific coasts there are areas of distinctive character of which the pre-Columbian populations seem to have taken full advantage—belts of mangrove swamp pierced by a network of tidal channels. These low-lying areas, teeming with fish and crustaceans, are particularly rich in shellfish, which can easily be gathered at low tide. The shell mounds, often of great size, which are found along the coasts at certain points are in fact so many gigantic refuse heaps. Moreover the high salinity of the lagoons often led to the establishment of salt-pans in these areas in pre-Hispanic times.

To complete this schematic inventory of resources we may note that gold is to be found in the upper valleys of the rivers which rise in some of the ancient ranges of crystalline rock, particularly in several areas in Panama. in the cordillera of Talamanca in Costa Rica, and in central Honduras, Unlike the Maya country (Petén and Yucatán), Central America is on the whole poorly supplied with soft limestone—a factor which in some cases may have impeded the development of architecture.

ETHNOHISTORY AND PREHISTORY

II

The native cultures of Central America did not long survive the brutal shock of the Spanish conquest and the colonisation which followed. It is estimated that over two thirds of the Indian population were wiped out between 1519 and 1650. Paradoxical as it may seem at first sight, it was the more backward and "primitive" cultures which maintained themselves longest, living as they did in the relative safety of areas which offered little attraction to Europeans.

The ethnographical study of Central America began with its discovery on Columbus's fourth voyage, and further material was contributed by the Conquistadors or missionaries or officials who recorded their observations of the native peoples, either in official reports or in writings intended for a wider audience. As early as the 16th century, too, we have the works of historians who, although they never set foot in the New World, were able to draw on eye-witness accounts by men who had taken part in expeditions to the West Indies. The very pirates might sometimes contribute their quota of useful information.

In the 19th century the ethnohistorians (i.e., ethnographers working on the basis of historical documents) began to collect material and subject it to critical analysis. Meanwhile the store of knowledge was being continually increased by the accounts brought back from their travels by diplomats, botanists, geologists and others, some of which are still of outstanding value.

The work of the ethnohistorians has been reinforced by that of the linguists who study the dictionaries and grammars compiled by missionaries and the vocabularies brought back by travellers. The comparative study of this material allows them to establish a classification of the native languages into groups, families and so on, and to cooperate with the ethnohistorians in seeking to define the territorial limits of the languages or language groups which they identify.

Studies of this kind frequently come up against unsurmountable difficulties, for the information available for particular areas or in particular fields varies widely in amount and quality. For most of the native peoples we have only the sketchiest of data on subjects which regularly show considerable variations from one people to another. In one area, for example, a traveller may have noted certain features which particularly struck him —the local ornaments, or methods of cooking, or fishing techniques. Elsewhere the same visitor, or some other traveller, may have observed merely some tribal ceremony or the local war customs. Thus in dealing with some particular subject the ethnohistorian will often have to rely on a very meagre supply of information gleaned from a considerable extent of territory. It is as a rule impossible to compare lists of cultural traits as between one ethnic group and another, or between one region or area and another, on account of the large gaps which such lists would show. On the other, hand, the few detailed descriptions of certain groups (e.g., the Nicarao) which we do possess may distort the perspective; for these cultures tend to appear richer than others merely because they are better documented.

But, however incomplete, the picture we can build up in this way of the native peoples of Central America in the 16th century is nevertheless of fundamental importance to the archaeologist. It provides the starting point of many of his enquiries and influences the formulation and definition of many of his problems. Moreover ethnohistorical and ethnographic studies can contribute to the solution of problems which arise in the interpretation of archaeological data. The archaeologists have always realised this, and from the outset their published work devoted much attention to the ethnohistory of the region or area concerned. On the face of it this was an entirely acceptable approach, but only if the data was considered in its chronological setting—that is, the post-Conquest period. It must be recognised that the results of excavation can only rarely be brought into association with the work of the historians; and when this possibility exists the greatest care is necessary in taking advantage of it. Up to the present the main contributions made by ethnography and historical linguistics have lain in formulating rather than in solving problems; their chief value is that they define for us in general outline the pattern of Central America in the 16th century, before the profound changes brought about by the Spanish colonisation.

Central America in the 16th Century

At the time of the Conquest the four main linguistic groups found in Mexico and Guatemala were also represented in Central America:
— the *Otomangue* group (Otomi, Mixtec, Zapotec, etc.) by the Chorotega-Mangue languages spoken on the Pacific coast of Honduras, Nicaragua Costa Rica;
— the *Hokaltec* group by Subtiaba in north-western Nicaragua and "Jicaque" in northern Honduras east of the Río Ulúa;
— the *Uto-Aztec* group by language families of the Nahua group—Pipil (western Salvador and north-western Honduras), Nicarao (southern Pacific area of Nicaragua) and Nahuatl or Aztec, spoken by small colonies of traders scattered about Honduras, El Salvador and Nicaragua; and
— the *Macro-Maya* group by Pokomam (of the Maya language family), spoken to the west of the Río Lempa in El Salvador.

Apart from a few Aztec enclaves and the Jicaques, all the tribes speaking these languages lived on the Pacific side of Central America, from El Salvador to the Nicoya peninsula. All the other languages of Central America belong to the large *Macro-Chibcha* group, with an area of distribution extending into Colombia. This group includes in particular three languages which at the time of the Conquest were spoken in the Pacific zone of northern Central America—Corobici (north-western Costa Rica), Ulva (southern Honduras) and Lenca (eastern Salvador, central and north-western Honduras).

In short, apart from these Chibcha intrusions, the languages of the northern Pacific zone are mostly of northern origin and give it its distinctive individuality.

How far does the evidence of ethnohistory confirm that of linguistics? Did the native cultures of this Pacific zone at the time of the Conquest differ from the other cultures of Central America? Does the ethnographic information suggest other subdivisions? These questions are difficult to answer, largely because of the general inadequacy and unevenness of our evidence. The available material does, however, suggest that the cultures of Central America, taken as a whole, show a certain degree of unity. No doubt this is because the isthmus—that narrow area in which population groups of different origins have lived side by side for thousands of years —has played the part of a melting pot. Are we then entitled to talk of a "Central American culture"?

We can discern certain common features in the pattern of such a culture. The Indians of Central America were basically farmers who cultivated maize, sweet manioc, beans, gourds, chili peppers, sweet potatoes and cacao, together with various species of fruit tree, tobacco and cotton. The crops were sown on ground prepared by burning: an area of forest was marked out, the trees were felled with stone axes, and the timber was burned on the spot. For plants reproduced by vegetative propagation like sweet potato and manioc the farmer built up low mounds of earth on which shoots were planted out. For seed plants like maize the sower made a hole in the ground with a planting stick, deposited a few seeds in it and drew soil over them with his foot; he then moved on a pace, repeated the process, and continued in the same way. After two or three harvests, when the yield began to fall, the field was abandoned and left fallow for a period of at least five years; a new plot was marked out to replace it, and so the process went on.

Apart from a few groups on the Caribbean coast, the population of the isthmus was a settled one, living in villages and hamlets. Political organisation had not advanced beyond the chiefdom stage, in which several villages were combined under the authority of a *cacique*. There was no building in stone: nothing but a few simple structures of timber or thatch standing on platforms of earth. The largest of these platforms were occupied by temples or chiefs' houses. Clothing, which varied considerably from one tribe to another, was woven from cotton or made of pounded bark fibre. The practice of body painting and tattooing was widespread, as was the wearing of gold ornaments (usually round the neck), which at once excited the covetousness of the Conquistadors. The invaders were also struck by the ear ornaments, sometimes of extraordinary size, made of semi-precious stones (jadeite, serpentine, agate, etc.), and by the rich necklaces, pendants and headdresses (in which much use was made of feathers). Implements were of wood, bone and above all of flaked or polished stone; metal was reserved for use in jewellery. Most of the vessels used were of pottery, fashioned without the use of a wheel and often decorated with modelled, incised or painted ornament. The commonest weapon, sometimes used for hunting and fishing as well as for war, was the bow. The main object of war, which seems to have been endemic everywhere, was the capture of prisoners, who were destined for sacrifice to the gods, and often eaten. The divinities were represented by idols of wood, metal or stone, which were worshipped in temples and were honoured by the slaughter of victims, by presents, and by offerings of the worshippers' own blood.

Many of these peoples discovered by the Spaniards at the beginning of the 16th century were found to be hierarchical societies organised in classes (chiefs and priests, warriors, ordinary people and slaves), with a developed system of craft production based on a highly organised division of labour and regular commercial exchanges. Even so, however, they had the appearance of poor relations in comparison with the Mesoamerican and Andean civilizations.

Although at first sight the pattern of Central America at the time of the Conquest seems to be fairly uniform, divergences begin to appear as soon as we look more closely at the evidence. When we attempt to draw lines of division, to compare the various cultural zones with one another, we end up with a picture entirely consistent with the results of linguistic study to which reference has already been made. The Pipil, Nicarao and Chorotega cultures of the Pacific zone show a number of features borrowed from the higher cultures of the north which set them apart from the other cultures of Central America. The most important differences are set out in the following table:

Pacific Zone	*Elsewhere*
Settlements tend to be concentrated	Settlements tend to be scattered
Houses occupied by single families	Houses occupied by several families
Agricultural work done by men	Agricultural work done by women
Maize pancakes *(tortillas)*	Maize loaves
Shamanism non-existent or undeveloped	Shamanism well developed
Confession	Not known
Solar calendar (365 days: $18 \times 20 + 5$)	Lunar calendar
Screen-fold books	Not known
Dances of northern origin (e.g. the *Volador*)	Not known
Patrilineal or bilateral filiation	Matrilineal filiation
Specialised markets	Not known
Cacao beans as money	Not known

But although it is thus possible to identify a Pacific zone with distinctive features of its own, the historical information available is too scanty and incomplete to permit us to recognise any other divisions in 16th century Central America[2]. The distinction between two different zones of influence, however, provides archaeological research with an important starting point. The questions which will arise in the course of our study will largely be concerned with the relationships between these two zones, and also between the peripheral areas and the centres of civilization.

HUAQUEROS AND
ARCHAEOLOGISTS

III

The treasure-hunters, amateur excavators and tomb-robbers (known from Costa Rica to Peru as *huaqueros*) are invariably earlier in the field than the archaeologists; and this rule—to which there are regrettably few exceptions—is particularly well illustrated in Central America.

The plundering of ancient burial places seems to have begun at least as early as the beginning of the 19th century. The rich tombs in Panama and Costa Rica, with their gold jewellery, were the first to attract the attention of the robbers, and the treasures found in them were rapidly melted down for the sake of the precious metal. At a later stage this developed into a regular trade in pre-Columbian antiquities, the chief purchasers being museums and private collectors in the United States, who were anxious to acquire not only jewellery but pieces of stone sculpture, jadeite ornaments and pottery. In spite of the efforts made by some of the countries concerned to put an end to the plundering of archaeological sites, clandestine excavators still pursue their illicit activities in defiance of the regulations—sometimes, indeed, with the connivance of the authorities. The results have been particularly deplorable in Costa Rica and Panama, where the *huaqueros* have devastated not merely individual sites but whole areas, destroying the archaeological record for ever. No doubt some of the material discovered has been preserved; but as a rule we do not know its exact provenance, its associations or the circumstances in which it was found, and are thus deprived of the fundamental data required for any scientific study. Accordingly the large-scale operations of the *huaqueros* have resulted in stocking museums and private collections with hundreds of thousands of pieces of which as a rule practically nothing is known.

When the first studies of Central American archaeology were undertaken in the second half of the 19th century much material had already been brought to light, and the writers sought to make it more widely known by publishing descriptions and illustrations. The bibliography on Panama between 1860 and 1900, for example, is relatively abundant, most of the articles being concerned with gold objects found by *huaqueros* or by the writers themselves in the tombs of Chiriquí. From the same period date the first descriptions of the large sculpture of Nicaragua (Bovallius, Squier, Crawford). Some writers, however, went beyond mere description in their studies of some of the large collections, particularly of pottery. Their analyses, mainly of a stylistic character, led to the classification of the material in "classes" or "wares", characterised by one or more distinctive attributes (Holmes, MacCurdy, Lothrop). These attempts were of limited value in so far as their authors, lacking precise information about the material, were unable to take account of its exact provenance or relative age. They thus inevitably ran the risk of lumping together material belonging to different cultures. In these first studies of collections for which the essential documentation was not available the interpretations, even if they avoided the wilder flights of fancy, were of very limited scope —confining themselves to identifying certain themes in the iconography or drawing comparisons with other areas which were better known, like Mexico or Peru.

The Swedish archaeologist Carl Hartman played a pioneering part in the history of Central American archaeology. His excavations of cemeteries in Costa Rica (1896, 1897, 1903), published in 1901 and 1907, were the first which can properly be described as scientific. Although the main object of his work was to enrich the museums of Stockholm and later of Pittsburgh, it was carried out carefully and conscientiously, and the associations of objects and their exact locations were scrupulously recorded in his published reports, which are still essential works of reference. Like his predecessors—and unfortunately also like most of his successors during the following half century—Hartman paid little attention to chronology: in the cemetery of Orosí (Central Valley), for example, he records two different groups of pottery without drawing the conclusion—which is quite evident to a modern reader of his work—that one of them is earlier than the other.

In general, with one or two exceptions, scholars tended until about 1950 to deny the existence in Central America of any historical dimension: their writings implicitly assumed that all the archaeological remains belonged to the tribes found in the area at the time of the Conquest. The pottery and sculpture of southern Nicaragua were labelled Nicarao or Chorotega, the corresponding material found in the Central Valley of Costa Rica was inevitably known as Huetar, and so on. This kind of assimilation is dangerous, for it implies that the cultures of these areas have remained unchanged since a remote period, or that the areas were first settled in relatively recent times. These two hypotheses, which seem unlikely enough on the face of it, have been finally put out of court by later work. In a short article published in 1927 S. K. Lothrop drew attention to the existence at Cerro Zapote (El Salvador) of two archaeological levels separated by a layer of volcanic ash; the upper level was rich in polychrome sherds, while the lower level had none but yielded instead fragments of figurines showing striking affinity with the Pre-Classic figurines of the Valley of Mexico. The two kinds of pottery clearly belonged to different periods, and the site thus provided convincing evidence that El Salvador at least had an archaeological history. The tombs at Playa de los Muertos (Honduras), excavated by D. Popenoe in 1934, yielded pottery which was shown by Vaillant to have analogies with the Pre-Classic pottery of the Valley of Mexico: here again at least two different periods were represented on the same site.

Modern archaeological research began in 1936 with the expedition to north-western Honduras sponsored by the Smithsonian Institution and the University of Harvard. Paying careful attention to stratigraphic techniques, Strong, Kidder and Paul sought to establish the cultural sequence in a number of localities, basing themselves on the analysis of fragments of pottery found in the floors of houses or in midden areas. This time the excavations were not confined to cemeteries, and an attempt was made to establish a relative chronology on the basis of the stratigraphy and to compare the sequence thus obtained with other known sequences. Unfortunately the results of this work have been published only in the form of a preliminary report; and this is the case also with other important explorations in El Salvador.

From 1950 onwards most of the excavations were deliberately directed towards the solution of chronological problems. Archaeologists had at last begun to realise that in areas whose past is for all practical purposes unknown the first task must be to establish a chronological and geographical framework. Only when the cultures have been properly located in time and space can the archaeologist set out to describe them without the risk of associating different groups of material which do not belong to the same culture.

Thus Central American archaeology, founded by Hartman at the end of the 19th century, made relatively little progress for almost fifty years thereafter. The splendid civilisations of Mesoamerica and the Andes quite naturally attracted the available financial resources and the efforts of the archaeologists, to the detriment of areas with a lower cultural level and less spectacular remains. Interest in Central America grew as the collections of material became richer; and when Lothrop was working on his study, *Pottery of Costa Rica and Nicaragua*, in the 1920s he was able to examine between 35,000 and 40,000 pieces of pottery in a number of different museums. And although for many years the great centres of civilisation were the magnets which attracted the main research effort there came a time when archaeologists began to take an interest in the history of events on the periphery of the "civilised" areas. Good work was done at a fairly early period in Honduras and El Salvador, mainly concerned with such problems as the definition of the "frontier" of the Maya area or of

Mesoamerica. It is significant also that the least known parts of the Inter-mediate Area are those which geographically are farthest from the early centres of civilisation.

Another reason for the reluctance of archaeologists to take an interest in Central America may perhaps be seen in the difficulty of this field, which often requires much effort to produce fairly meagre results. If Central American archaeology seems unrewarding to some scholars, this can be attributed to three main factors—the almost complete absence of building in stone, the scattered settlement pattern and the disappearance of perishable structures and materials in consequence of the general humidity of the climate.

Throughout most of the isthmus the sites are of small size, recognisable only by low mounds or by the occurrence of sherds of pottery on the surface. Excavation may reveal pottery or stone or metal objects; more rarely objects of shell or bone, which are less resistant to the passage of time. Buildings, wood implements, feather ornaments, cotton fabrics and bark paper, seeds and other material remains have perished beyond recovery. Confronted with these difficulties, the archaeologist who wants to be more than a mere *huaquero* must use and develop methods and techniques which enable him to make the best of a situation that has frustrated so many of his predecessors.

THEORY, PROBLEMS AND METHODS

IV

The characteristic feature of archaeology in the Americas is its close dependence on anthropology. There are historical reasons for this: in the United States, where American archaeology had its beginnings, the Indians and the relics of their ancestors were discovered at the same time. The study of the primitive peoples of America advanced in step with the study of the remains left by the peoples of the past. Accounts of the one merged easily into descriptions of the other, and there was a constant effort to establish a relationship between the results produced by the ethnographer and the archaeologist—who often, indeed, were the same person. Even in our own day archaeologists in the United States specialising in American archaeology are attached to the university departments of anthropology, and in France the study of American archaeology is centred on the Musée de l'Homme in Paris, a museum of anthropology.

In terms of theory the archaeologist-anthropologist attaches prime importance to the concept of *culture*. His aim is to discover in the surviving remains—understood in the widest sense—the result of certain types of behaviour, which must in turn be interpreted as the expression of certain ideas or norms which, taken as a whole and defined in time and space, make up the culture of a society.

For the specialist in American archaeology the fundamental unit is the *phase*, a grouping of cultural traits limited in space to a particular locality or region and in time to a relatively short duration. A phase comprises a certain number—and the number will vary according to the results obtained—of *complexes*, which classify the archaeological material into broad categories. Many phases are still defined only by the ceramic complex associated with them; others comprise a lithic complex, an architectural complex, a funerary complex, and so on. A chronological succession of phases is known as a *sequence*, which may be local or regional according to the geographical limits assigned to it.

Before setting out to establish in a particular region a sequence based on a detailed description of different cultural aspects at different periods, the archaeologist must begin with the most urgent requirement, which is to construct a sequence of ceramic complexes. Why, it may be asked, should he begin with the pottery? There are purely empirical reasons for this. Of all the remains of the past sherds of pottery are the most abundant, which makes it possible to use statistical methods; and they are to be found everywhere—in settlements and cemeteries, in fill material and on the surface. Moreover pottery is relatively durable, and is sufficiently complex in structure to offer a large number of attributes which can be used for the purposes of classification—differences of paste, of surface treatment, of form and decoration.

In field archaeology the ceramic sequence is usually obtained by the excavation of stratified deposits in midden or habitation areas. The sherds are gathered in natural *layers* or in arbitrary *levels* of constant thickness (10 or 20 cm.). Excavation in layers is an application of the geological principles of stratigraphy: the ceramic types found on a site are associated with particular geological strata or building stages or other historical accidents. The method of excavation in arbitrary levels, introduced in the United States by Nels Nelson in 1912, is based on an assumed relationship between changes in pottery type and relative depth, these changes being expressed by the relative frequencies of different pottery types at different levels. The ceramic sequence can also be obtained or completed by the method known as *seriation*, which involves arranging in chronological order, on the basis of the frequency of the ceramic types, deposits which show no stratigraphical relationship.

All these methods can yield the desired results only if they are based on a rigorous classification of the pottery. This is divided into *types*, which are units combining several *attributes* considered by the classifier to be significant. The main function of pottery types is to measure cultural variations in time and space, and the features adopted for the purpose of defining them must themselves be subject to change.

A ceramic sequence built up in this way provides only a relative chronology: it will tell us that complex B is later than complex C and earlier than complex A, but it will not give the absolute age of any of the complexes. For this purpose it is necessary to use absolute dating techniques, and in particular the carbon 14 method, the only method so far used in Central America. The charcoal or other organic material which is used for the laboratory tests must be associated with pottery of a particular level or deposit. A series of datings of samples from different stratigraphic levels or different deposits in a series will then make it possible to confirm the sequence and date the various divisions within it.

The ceramic sequence provides the chronological framework which is necessary before we can construct the cultural sequence. If, for example, we are studying the funerary customs of a particular site or region, the pottery associated with the burials will enable us to assign them to a particular phase. If we are interested in the settlement pattern the pottery found in the floors of houses will indicate the relative duration of occupancy of each house. The sherds found in the fill of buildings may not enable us to date the structures themselves, but they will at least indicate that the buildings cannot be earlier than the latest sherds associated with them. In this way the various evidences of material culture discovered by the archaeologist can be assigned by him to the different phases in the sequence with the help of the ceramic complexes; and he can then proceed to describe the cultural content of each phase and attempt to establish its chronological and geographical limits.

In the light of the foregoing discussion it is clear that archaeological research in Central America must be directed in the first place towards the solution of spatio-temporal problems. Before he embarks on a detailed study of the content of the prehistoric cultures of Central America the archaeologist must first have established the necessary chronological and geographical frameworks. Within a particular site or region the ceramic sequence makes it possible to group together the remains belonging to the same period. Within a wider geographical area the combination of a number of sequences provides a conspectus of the cultural development of the area. Thereafter —at some future date which we cannot yet foresee—it will be possible to fill out these frameworks, to put flesh on these skeletons, and to move on from description to interpretation.

FIRST RESULTS
OF CENTRAL AMERICAN
ARCHAEOLOGY

V

A glance at the select bibliography at the end of this volume will show that there are still serious gaps in our knowledge. Of the greater part of the territory we call Central America we know practically nothing, for the simple reason that there are still immense tracts unvisited by archaeologists—central and eastern Honduras, the whole of Nicaragua apart from the south-western part of the country, the eastern half of Costa Rica and Panama as far as the Canal, and the province of Darien which lies between the Canal and the Colombian frontier. Nor indeed can we claim to have any exact picture of the prehistory of the rest of Central America; for little of the work done there has been of adequate scientific standard, and much of it has been published in an unduly concise form which reduces its value.

As we have seen, ethnohistory and historical linguistics agree in distinguishing two contrasted areas in 16th century Central America—on the one hand a zone of Mesoamerican tradition and on the other the rest of the isthmus, basically of South American tradition. In our present state of knowledge this division still provides a valid basis for any account of the broad lines of cultural evolution before the arrival of Europeans in the area; and the available information allows us to go farther than this and subdivide the zone of Mesoamerican tradition into a northern and a southern sector.

In the following account the historical continuum is divided into a number of periods of sufficient length to accommodate the various phases, which can usually be dated only very broadly. The definition of these periods is based on our present knowledge, and there is no doubt that further work will make it possible in future to achieve a more precise and refined subdivision.

Zone of Mesoamerican Tradition

This area comprises El Salvador, western, central and southern Honduras, the western part of Nicaragua, and north-western Costa Rica as far as the 10th degree of latitude. The boundary between the northern and southern sectors of the zone runs on one side or other of the frontier between Honduras and Nicaragua, varying from period to period.

Although we have as yet no proofs of the antiquity of man in Central America, we have at least a number of indications:

— Two fluted projectile points (of a type which dates back between 10,000 and 12,000 years in the United States and South America) were found in a collection of material from north-western Costa Rica purchased by Hartman.

— Human footprints have been found in lava flows, covered by later deposits, in El Salvador and Nicaragua. The geologists cannot determine their age with any exactitude, but agree that the prints found in Nicaragua are not less than 5000 years old.

— An obsidian industry consisting of large flakes and points without fluting was found on the surface of a number of sites in central Honduras which yielded no pottery. These remains presumably belong to a pre-ceramic period, but their date is unknown.

The subsequent periods, associated in Mesoamerica with the first appearance and slow development of agriculture, the beginnings of settled life and the earliest occurrence of pottery, are not documented in the zone. It may be supposed that pottery was in use here from at least the beginning of the first millennium; for it is attested by 2000 B.C. both in Mexico (Tehuacán valley) and Panama (Monagrillo), and at least as early as 1300 B.C. on the Pacific coast of Guatemala (Ocós).

Period I (?–200 B.C.)

The oldest archaeological evidence we possess comes from excavations
—most of them carried out quite recently—in the northern sector of the
zone. This period takes in the ceramic complexes of Honduras, which
are shown by the stratigraphy to be earlier than the pottery with Usulután
decoration (see p. 40)—Yarumela I and II, Lo de Vaca I (Comayagua
valley) and Jaral (Los Naranjos, Lake Yojoa).

These various groups have a number of common features—their simplicity
of form, the small proportion of decorated pottery, the preponderance
of incised over painted decoration—but in other respects they show considerable divergences. The comparison with other known complexes of similar
date, particularly from the Maya Highlands and Lowlands, also gives
disappointing results: the pre-Usulután pottery is agreed to have Pre-Classic
affinities, even though it is not possible to cite a list of traits common
to two or more complexes attributed to the same period. Thus the diversity
of the pottery may reflect a high degree of cultural regionalism—indeed
of particularism. The detailed publication of the work done in this field
will no doubt make it possible to define this more exactly.

Apart from the pottery the only evidence we have on this period comes
from Los Naranjos. The site was then bounded by a defensive ditch about
1300 metres long, 15 to 20 metres wide and 7 metres deep. Starting from
Lake Yojoa, this ended at a pool to the north of the main group, where
within a platform 6 metres in height were found the remains of a personage
wearing various jadeite ornaments—a necklace, a belt made up of four rows
of beads, and two ear ornaments of unusually large size (12 cm. in diameter).
At the foot of the west side of the platform were found a number of burials
which contained no individual offerings but had associated with them as a
group a jadeite axe with a coating of cinnabar. This is strongly reminiscent

of practices recorded at La Venta, the great centre of the Olmec civilisation (first half of first millenium).

From these finds we can deduce that the Jaral phase had attained a higher cultural level than the simplicity of the pottery would suggest. The richness of one of the burials as compared with the others is the mark of a hierarchical society; the ditch and the platforms must represent a large-scale collective enterprise; and the construction of the ditch, which can only have had a defensive function, shows that the people of Los Naranjos were obliged to devote considerable efforts to maintaining their security.

At El Trapiche (near Chalchuapa, El Salvador) a long ceramic sequence has been obtained within the last few years. In the excavator's opinion three of the complexes which have been identified are earlier than 300 B.C. They can be compared with other Mesoamerican sequences, but there appears to be nothing corresponding to the complexes discovered in Honduras, which once again remain isolated.

A few miles from El Trapiche, at Las Victorias, four figures of indisputably Olmec character were found carved on a boulder. They are shown in profile, with jaguar-like mouths and wearing the typical Olmec "football helmet" and a pectoral. One of them is wearing a wing-like cloak and is carrying what has been interpreted as a club but seems in fact to be a "standard" *(Pl. 1)*. The boulder at Las Victorias is the most southerly example of Olmec monumental art. It must be considered along with the influences from the same civilisation which have been recognised at Los Naranjos; but further work is required to determine the importance of these features.

Period II

In this period the boundary between the two sectors lies approximately on the latitude of Managua (Nicaragua).

Northern Sector (200 B.C. to 550 A.D.)

In 1965 excavations in the Choluteca valley (southern Honduras) showed no discontinuity between a complex of Pre-Classic affinities and another manifestly of "Late Classic" character (Baudez, 1966). Similar results obtained in the same year at Lo de Vaca (Comayagua valley) were confirmed three years later at Los Naranjos. The stratigraphy obtained in various excavations at this site provides a more substantial foundation for the hypothesis put forward after the 1965 excavations. If there is no interruption between the pottery which is identified on typological grounds as Pre-Classic and that which is shown to be of Late Classic period, this is because the former persisted throughout the period corresponding to the Early Classic of Mesoamerica (250-550 A.D.).

While polychrome pottery appears in the Maya area as early as the 2nd century, it is another 400 years before evidence of this ware is found in the neighbourhood of Lake Yojoa or the Comayagua depression. The preliminary results do not point to any great changes in the pottery during a period estimated at almost eight centuries. It must be the task of further analysis to identify criteria sufficiently sensitive to the passage of time to permit the subdivision of a period of such considerable length.

We may conclude from the preceding discussion that the north-western part of Central America remained free of Maya influence until the 6th century. If there had been any contacts other than purely accidental ones between the Maya and their neighbours to the south they would have left some traces in the pottery of these peoples. The only possible exception to this isolation of the northern sector during the Early Classic period might perhaps be looked for in western Salvador. At Tazumal (Chalchuapa region) an early phase antedating the building of Structure I is rather sketchily defined on the basis of a relatively small number of items. Some of these pieces show close affinities with Maya pottery of the Early Classic period *(Pl. 28)*.

The pottery of this period from the various sites in central Honduras shows a certain unity. The decorative techniques include incision (alone or in combination with painting, in the style known as "Zoned Painting"), impressed ornament (shell-impressions and rocker-stamping), punctation and bichrome painting (with very simple linear elements painted in red on buff, or black on red). Whether the decoration is painted, impressed or incised, or in relief (with appliqué motifs) the patterns are usually geometrical, and where occasionally there is an attempt at representation it is highly stylised. There are, however, certain jars in human or animal form in which the head and body are modelled and certain features like wings or feet are indicated by incision or painting.

The distinctive features of the complex belonging to the Chismuyo phase of southern Honduras (with a carbon 14 dating of 370 ± 100 A.D.) are the corrugations on the necks of the jars and the groups of wavy lines incised with a toothed instrument. It is also distinguished from the ceramic complexes of central Honduras by the absence of rocker stamping and Zoned Bichrome decoration.

In spite of these local differences, all the ceramic complexes of the northern sector during this period are marked by the absence of polychrome ware and the considerable quantity of orange-coloured ware decorated in the Usulután technique. This decoration consists of parallel lines, usually wavy, in light colours against a darker background, which seem as a rule to be obtained by drawing a toothed instrument over a freshly slipped or smoked surface. The pottery with Usulután decoration shows a great variety of form—jars with and without handles, sometimes with a spout, with a flat or pointed or depressed base, or with three or four feet; tripod or tetrapod bowls (Pl. 2, 3), or bowls with an annular base; dishes with a flared rim; anthropomorphic or zoomorphic jars (Pl. 4, 5); "pot-stands"; effigy vases (Pl. 7); and statuettes. The Usulután decoration is often associated with other ornamental techniques—incision (Pl. 6), fluting, impressing, white or red painting, etc.

40

2, 3

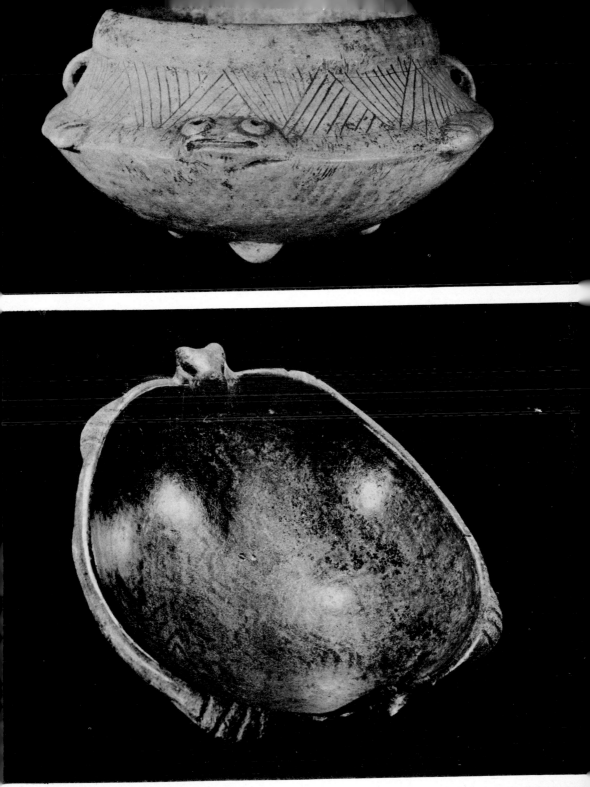

4, 5

13

16

20

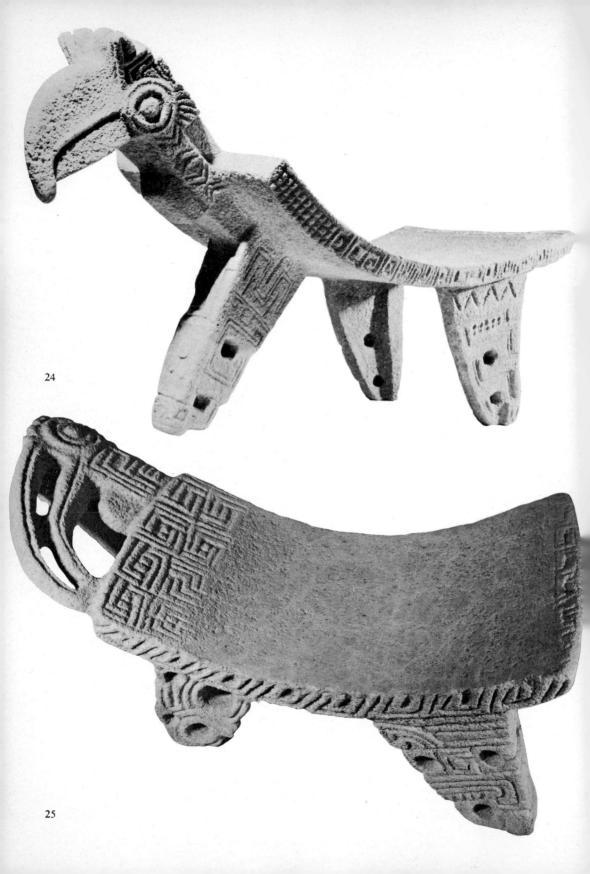

24

25

The Usulután decoration is important because of its wide distribution in space and time. It is found in varying proportions from southern Mexico to northern Nicaragua, but seems to have been most popular in western Salvador and at Copán. From its first appearance in the 2nd century B.C. it continues to occur in the Maya area throughout a period of some five centuries. Farther south, however, it evidently maintained its popularity for another three hundred years or more. It provides another example of a trait of chronological relevance in the area of the "higher cultures" which can be accepted as a "horizon marker" in that area, but elsewhere loses all significance for that purpose.

There are numerous sites dating from this period, with the remains of both ceremonial centres and mere villages.

At Los Naranjos the main group of monuments consists of seven large mounds ranging in height between 3 and 19 metres. The two most imposing structures so far explored belong for the most part to the Eden phase. Structure I was then a stepped pyramid some 18 metres high. Structure IV consisted of a stepped platform surmounted by four structures aligned on the cardinal points and enclosing a rectangular open space or *plaza;* it was approached from the west by a ramp made of blocks of undressed stone laid flat on the surface of the slope. Structure IV was built almost entirely of earth, apart from the ramp and the retaining walls of the steps of the platform and the structures, which were of undressed limestone blocks bonded with clay. No trace of any surface rendering, either of stucco or cement, was found. A second defensive ditch some 5 km. long was dug during the Eden phase. This was 4 metres deep and 8 to 15 metres wide, with an earthwork 2 metres high along the south-western edge. Unlike the first ditch, which took in little more than the main group of structures, this enclosed a considerable area of fertile land.

At Yarumela the largest mounds (over 10 metres in height) appear to date from this period, on the evidence of the pottery which litters the surface.

They are rectangular stepped platforms approached by staircases (or ramps?) and aligned on the cardinal points. At El Trapiche (El Salvador) Structure I, a mound 20 metres high in the centre of the site, dominates an open space which is bounded on the south by a row of three rectangular mounds.

The size and concentration of the structures on these three sites suggest that they were probably ceremonial centres used by a population living in scattered villages in the surrounding area. The villages themselves consist of low platforms, usually not more than a metre high, on which the houses were built; but since the houses, like the temples, were constructed of perishable materials, no trace of them has survived. The village of Lo de Vaca, which was occupied during the following period as well, consists of several dozen house sites, but has only one mound of larger size, several metres in height. It is likely that the inhabitants of Lo de Vaca, only 4 miles from Yarumela, took part—at any rate on special occasions—in the activities of the ceremonial centre, as well as in its building and maintenance. Farther south, in the Choluteca valley, there seems to have been nothing comparable with Los Naranjos or Yarumela, to judge by the unpretentious nature of the structures dating from this period. At La Barranca there is a group of ten oval or circular platforms, ranging in height from 1 to 2½ metres, arranged in a circle round the highest of the group—no doubt a small temple or chief's house.

We know little about other manifestations of these cultures, the study of which is only just beginning. The frequent occurrence of basalt *metates* (grinding stones) suggests that this was a population of farmers, who also (on the evidence of obsidian and flint spear points) engaged in hunting, and probably in food-gathering and fishing as well. They wore clothing of cotton or bark cloth, as is indicated by the spindle whorls and the beaters for pounding the bark which were found in the excavations. The art of sculpture seems to have been little developed; but this impression may arise merely from the difficulty of assigning certain pieces to a particular period. We can, however, date to this period two fragments of stelae, one from Yarumela and the other from El Trapiche, as well as some curious mushroom-shaped pieces of sculpture which are common on the Pacific coast of Guatemala and are found also in El Salvador.

There are also widely distributed pottery figurines, almost invariably nude figures of women, whose function is difficult to determine (Pl. 9, 10). They are of solid construction (unlike the figurines of later periods, which are often hollow), of varying size (from 10 to 30 cm. in height) and sometimes painted white or orange in Usulután decoration (Pl. 11). The features are indicated very simply in incised or relief form, and most of the pieces show striking affinities with the Pre-Classic figurines of Mesoamerica. Although some of them no doubt date from the Pre-Classic period many others have been found in association with material which is certainly later, and thus provide another example of "Archaic" survivals in the northern sector. The best known of the figurines are those in the style which is well illustrated at Playa de los Muertos: they are of outstanding aesthetic quality, a quality which results partly from their graceful proportions and partly from their charm of attitude and expression, which are rendered with great restraint (Pl. 8).

These cultures show a degree of complexity which was for long unsuspected. They were clearly hierarchical societies, sufficiently prosperous to be able to devote a considerable surplus of production to the service of the gods.

Since we are unable in the present state of knowledge to subdivide the long stretch of time—some eight centuries—covered by Period II, we do not know whether the cultures described had the same characteristics from the beginning of the Late Pre-Classic period or whether some of these features—perhaps even most of them—were the result of a long period of evolution, or of external influences which cannot be identified in the pottery. The solution of these problems must surely be one of the priorities for the future.

Southern Sector (300 B.C. to 500 A.D.)

Within the last ten years or so sites in this sector have been investigated by a number of expeditions, both European and American. Unfortunately the results of this work, except in one case, are known only from preliminary reports.

A cultural sequence valid for the whole of the sector has been built up from various local sequences. It begins with the "Zoned Bichrome" period, the estimated dates of which are 300 B.C. to 300 A.D.[3]. The name comes from the characteristic type of decoration, which is common to all the various ceramic complexes included in the period. This consists of various combinations of painted and incised decoration—alternating groups of incised straight lines and areas painted in red *(Pl. 15)* or areas painted red on a buff ground, or black on red, or black and red on buff, the painted surfaces being delineated by an incised line. A simple bichrome decoration is very common, consisting of elementary geometric motifs (parallel straight lines, triangles or chevrons) painted in black on a red ground or in red on a buff ground; this is found on bowls and even more commonly on jars. Several types show incised or impressed decoration, including shell impressions, zoned punctation and incised motifs. Usulután pottery is so rare that it seems likely to have been an import.

The shapes include jars *(Pl. 12)*, shallow or hemispherical bowls, usually with three feet, squat composite-silhouette jars, bottle-shaped jars *(Pl. 13)*, footed cylindrical jars with a rim under the lip *(Pl. 16)*, zoomorphic jars and pot-stands *(Pl. 17)*. Figurines, unpainted and decorated only with incised and appliqué ornament, have been recorded only in Nicaragua. In Costa Rica, however, some large statuettes of seated female figures have been found, sometimes showing close affinities with the figurines decorated in the Usulután style found in northern Nicaragua and El Salvador. They are hollow, with a "Zoned Bichrome" decoration *(Pl. 18)*.

Spherical ocarinas, with from four to eight holes, are commonly found throughout the whole of the sector. They are decorated at one or both ends with modelled animal heads, usually birds, and are made of fine paste, with a highly polished surface decorated with incised lines and areas of very delicate punctation done with the edge of a shell *(Pl. 14)*.

The subsequent period, known as "Linear Decorated", is so far represented only by the Ciruelas phase of the Tempisque valley sequence. Its estimated dates (300-500 A.D.) bring it into approximate correspondence with the Early Classic of Mesoamerica. The ceramic complex includes types which had already appeared during the previous period but achieved their greatest popularity in the Ciruelas phase, together with some new types. Of the former group the most important is the Guinea Incised type, consisting mainly of tripod bowls and small squat jars made of fine paste, with a well burnished orange-red surface. The decoration is mainly incised (bands of geometric motifs), but also uses punctation, modelling and appliqué motifs. Frequently the vessels represent animals—mostly birds *(Pl. 21)*, but also peccaries, tapirs, coatis, crocodiles, monkeys and jaguars—which are indicated in relief by the head and one or two of the main features (wings, legs or tail). Genuinely zoomorphic vases (i.e., reproducing the form of the animal) and vases representing complex scenes are rare *(Pl. 20)*. The Guinea style is also found in statuettes *(Pl. 19)*, whistles and ocarinas of this period, decorated with appliqué pellets and fillets.

The bichromes (mainly black on red) of the earlier period are now supplemented by important innovations which substantially enrich the repertoire of painted decoration. The Zelaya Trichrome type consists of large-mouthed jars with pronounced shoulders, the rim and lower part of which are painted red, while the neck is left in buff with a decoration of vertical black lines drawn with a toothed instrument. The polychrome jars of López and Nosará type have black geometric motifs edged with a white line on a red ground *(Pl. 22)*.

The sites belonging to the Zoned Bichrome and Linear Decorated periods are few in number, and the population seems to have been low during these periods. The houses of the little hamlet of Ortega (Tempisque valley) were built on the natural ground surface round a rocky knoll, 2 metres high, which is littered with sherds and may have been the site of a dwelling or a temple. La Bocana, a site which was occupied during the Zoned Bichrome period, is a small cave, but large enough to have provided accommodation for a family; this type of occupation seems to have been exceptional, and most of the population must have lived in villages and hamlets. Like their neighbours in the northern sector, they lived from the produce of agriculture, combined with fishing, hunting and food-gathering, and knew the art of weaving. We know of two Zoned Bichrome burials —one at Chahuite Escondido (Costa Rica), containing the bodies of children buried in urns, and the other at Palmar (Nicaragua), where the skeleton of an adult was found lying on its back, with the skull resting on a *metate* and covered by an upturned bowl.

We have, however, a good deal of information about burials of the Linear Decorated period as a result of the excavation of the Bolson and Las Huacas cemeteries. In the former, which occupies the top of a natural hill in the Tempisque valley, the remains of twelve burials were found. Most of these were secondary burials (i.e., bundles of bones brought together for burial after the removal of the flesh from the bodies), but a number of skeletons in a seated position were also discovered. The offerings deposited with the bodies consist mainly of pottery, together with accidental occurrences of a small undecorated *metate*, some ocarinas and a few jadeite beads.

Most of the tombs in the cemetery of Las Huacas (near Nicoya), which was excavated by Hartman at the end of the 19th century, have recently been assigned to the Linear Decorated period on the strength of the pottery of this period which was found in them. The material in this cemetery is incomparably richer than at Bolson: there is relatively little pottery, but instead there are jadeite ornaments, mace-heads of hard stone and zoomorphic *metates* of basalt with an elaborate decoration which suggests that they were intended for ceremonial use. The *metate*, a concave rectangular slab carried on three rectangular legs, which in some cases are perforated, has at one end the head of a jaguar or a bird *(Pl. 24, 25)*. The under surface of the slab is decorated with bas-reliefs, sometimes representing the body of a bird whose head is depicted on one of the legs. The mace-heads carved from jadeite, nephrite, chalcedony, jasper and other stones are usually in the shape of animals' heads *(Pl. 27)*. The ornaments of jadeite—which *huaqueros* have recently found in association with Zoned Bichrome pottery in a cemetery near Santa Cruz—and other semi-precious stones consist mainly of rectangular pendants representing stylised birds or human beings *(Pl. 26)*. The decorated *metates* and jadeite ornaments continued to be popular in later periods.

Las Huacas does not merely give us information about the excellence of the local craftsmanship and the elaboration of the objects intended for ornament or for cult purposes. The contrast between the wealth of Las Huacas and the unpretentious burials of Bolson—two places no more than 15 miles apart—reflects either a class difference (nobles or priests on the one hand, ordinary people on the other) or some local difference of function—perhaps between the chief town of a district or a political and ceremonial centre on the one hand and a modest hamlet on the other.

In the present state of our knowledge the southern sector has the appearance in Period II (300 B.C. to 500 A.D.) of an area of transition between regions belonging to the Mesoamerican tradition and others of South American tradition. The pottery shows more influences from the south than from the north, but we are not yet in a position to decide, except on an entirely arbitrary basis, that the sector can be assigned to any particular sphere of influence[4].

Period III

As in the preceding period, the boundary between the two sectors can be drawn in the latitude of Managua.

Northern Sector (550-950 A.D.)

During the Late Classic period—the most brilliant period of Maya civilisation—the northern sector, now under the influence of its neighbours, reached its peak. Most of the sites in El Salvador and Honduras date from this period, indicating a substantial increase in population.

The site of Tazumal comprises some ten low mounds, a ball court and the imposing Structure I, the present height of which is about 15 metres *(Pl. 29)*. This consists of two pyramidal stepped platforms, one on top of the other; the top was originally occupied by a temple, of which hardly any trace now remains. The excavators identified six building phases for the lower platform and at least three for the upper one. The temple was approached from the west by way of a staircase flanked by balustrades. The structure is built of adobe bricks or stone, bound with clay, with an external facing in a cement-like material. The ball court, which has not been excavated, lies between two parallel mounds aligned from east to west and is bounded at the western end by a low platform or wall.

On the north side of Lake Yojoa (Los Naranjos and other sites) there was a larger population during the Yojoa phase than in earlier periods. At Los Naranjos itself, although relatively few changes were made in the main group, we can see evidence elsewhere on the site of considerable building activity on structures of modest size.

Tenampua, farther south in the Comayagua valley, is a good example of a fortified site. It occupies the top of a steep-sided hill, the natural defences

28

29

31

32

33

34

40

41

42

51

60

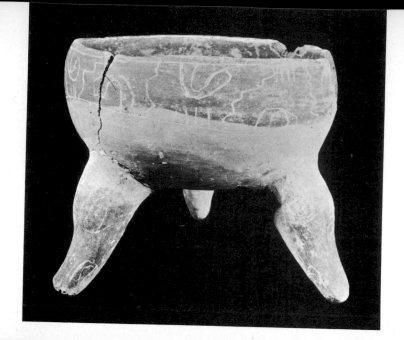

61

being strengthened by walls of undressed stone. It comprises something like a hundred separate structures, divided into several groups. In the centre is a rectangular space 100 metres long, bounded by a wall which has an opening on the west side; and within this enclosure are three of the largest mounds on the site. A short distance away is a ball court open on two sides. Although Tenampua has never been excavated by professional archaeologists, we can judge that the building techniques were fairly primitive, with undressed stone, ramps instead of staircases, no external rendering, and so on. Of the many other sites of the same period in the Comayagua valley none seems to have been of similar importance to Tenampua; it seems likely, therefore, that it was the political or religious centre for the villages and hamlets in the valley, taking over the function previously performed by Yarumela.

The ball court of Los Llanitos (eastern Salvador) is the most southerly structure of the type so far known. It is in the shape of a capital I, bounded to east and west by two platforms built of earth and roughly dressed blocks of basalt. The site also comprises some ten mounds, the highest of which (from 2 to 5.60 metres) stand in a line to the south of the ball court. Beyond Los Llanitos and Quelepa, where excavations are at present in progress, no site of comparable importance, either in extent or in the number of mounds, has been recorded. The only known sites are the remains of small villages, of which Buena Vista (Choluteca valley) may be taken as an example: here numbers of house platforms less than a metre in height are arranged in two concentric rings round three structures with a height of some 3 metres. Thus as we proceed from north to south the sites become smaller, the structures are lower, and specialised architectural units like the ball court tend to disappear.

At the beginning of the period which corresponds chronologically to the beginnings of the Tepeu phase in the Maya Lowlands the pottery, which for many centuries had tirelessly repeated itself, underwent radical changes, and new shapes, decorative techniques and themes suddenly took the place of the older ones. Polychrome decoration in particular appears in fully mature form from its very first occurrence. It does not appear to be preceded by any of the fumblings, the first uncertain efforts, of an art developing on its own. As soon as it appears it is fully adult; and this implies that it had been brought in from elsewhere. This does not mean that the polychrome pottery of Honduras and El Salvador is Maya, or a poor copy of Maya work: it suggests merely that these very individual styles, sometimes producing work of high quality, which occur alongside the others found in the northern sector were developed mainly on the basis of elements borrowed from the Maya.

The Copador type is very common in western Salvador and at Copán. The most popular shapes are bowls, decorated in red, purple and black on a light buff ground *(Pl. 31)*. The principal themes are animals (birds, monkeys) and, even more frequently, human figures, represented conventionally in a seated position or lying flat *(Pl. 30)*. The upper part of the vessel has frequently a decorative frieze made up of elements which are clearly imitated from Maya glyphs. These "false glyphs" are often used also in the decoration of polychrome vases (black and red on a light brown ground) of other types, long known as "Mayoid", from El Salvador and Honduras *(Pl. 32, 33)*, depicting mythological animals *(Pl. 34)* and men in processional formation, either standing or seated. Some vases, usually cylindrical in shape with tripod supports, depict quite complex scenes, which we are usually unable to interpret in detail but which clearly represent political events (a dignitary receiving the homage of subjects or vassals, or a meeting between two dignitaries and their retinues) or religious ceremonies (dancing or the making of offerings) *(Pl. 35-38, 39, 41)*. In the Ulúa valley, and to an even greater extent in the area round Lake Yojoa, representations of animals are found in great quantity, the commonest subjects being birds (herons, cranes, owls and vultures), jaguars and monkeys *(Pl. 42, 43)*. Monkeys' heads modelled in relief are frequently found on polychrome cylindrical vases or on jars painted in a single colour *(Pl. 44, 46)*. At Tenampua, which has yielded the finest painted pottery in the whole zone, excavation brought to light an unusual type of cylindrical vase with three twisted feet, decorated with a combination of polychrome painting and the spikes usually found only on incense-burners *(Pl. 45)*.

The Ulúa-Yojoa polychrome pottery of Honduras, with its Salvadorian variants, is found also in northern Nicaragua. It comprises some very individual styles, in which, however, we can recognise borrowings from Maya pottery of the end of the Early Classic period and the Late Classic period—in the shapes (flat-bottomed cylindrical vases, cylindrical vases with three rectangular feet *(Pl. 47)*, barrel-shaped jars, composite-silhouette bowls, etc.), the techniques (black and red painting on a light brown or orange ground) and the subject matter ("false glyphs", processions of figures in ritual attitudes, scenes of political or religious life). There are also monochrome hemispherical bowls or cylindrical vases with carved bands of "false glyphs", again showing Maya influence *(Pl. 49)*. Other examples are the cylindrical incense-burners with rectangular "wings", decorated with a mask or a figure in relief, and the jadeite plaques found at Tazumal.

Other Mesoamerican influences can be detected. A jar from Tenampua bears the conventional representation of the jaws of Tlaloc, the Mexican rain god *(Pl. 45)*. Although it is clear that this theme had its origin in Mexico, we may still speculate by what roundabout route it reached the Comayagua valley and how many changes it underwent in the process. The same questions may be asked about the handsome marble vases from the Ulúa valley decorated with volutes in relief reminiscent of the Classic style of Veracruz, the area of origin of the few specimens of *hachas* and *palmas* (thought to be associated with the ceremonial of the ball game) which are found in western Salvador and on the Pacific coast of Guatemala *(Pl. 50, 51)*.

Although we know that the archaeology of the northern sector between 550 and 950 A.D. shows strong influences from the Mesoamerican civilisations, and particularly from the Maya, we have no idea at all of the precise source of these influences (a single site like Copán, or some particular region, or several different regions?) or by what route and in what form (commercial or religious? through the intermediary of merchants or missionaries? by peaceful or warlike means? in a provincial or colonial form?) they were transmitted.

Whatever may be the answers to these questions, however, it is clear that during the period of Maya influence the northern sector reached its apogee. The population increased, new villages were established, political and ceremonial centres were founded and maintained with the help of an abundant labour force, and temples were erected on the summit of pyramids. Artists and craftsmen reached a high peak of technical and aesthetic achievement and their products were distributed over long distances by the merchants. The paintings they have left us on their vases introduce us to a highly hierarchised society, performing the complex rituals of their religion.

In spite of these achievements, some of them of a very high order, we cannot regard the cultures of the northern sector as belonging to the Classic Maya civilisation. This is partly because they lack some of the fundamental and characteristic features of that civilisation, like the corbelled vault used in Maya architecture, the practice of periodically erecting carved stone stelae bearing dates and other inscriptions, and the art of writing — for the only glyphs known here are decorative features and not meaningful symbols. But it is also because these cultures are seen to be of merely marginal importance, in so far as their finest achievements are quantitatively and qualitatively inferior to those of the Maya. Their sites are fewer in number and smaller in size; and the specialised structures—also fewer in number and much smaller—show the use of relatively primitive techniques.

In terms of the total number of man-hours required, the size of the labour force employed at one time, and the energy and skill involved in their construction, these structures fall far short of the effort involved in the building of a Maya temple.

Finally we may wonder to what extent some of the more spectacular developments in the northern sector during this period are due to Maya influences. It must be remembered that many cultural traits formerly considered as Maya are already present in Period II—for example the contrast between larger centres and mere villages or hamlets, the concentration of the most important specialised structures, the alignment of such structures on the cardinal points round rectangular or square *plazas*, the use of stepped platforms as the substructures of temples, the "acropolises" or groups of structures built on platforms, etc.

Southern Sector (500-800 A.D.)

In Costa Rica and Nicaragua the Early Polychrome period has been dated between 500 and 800 A.D. on the basis of a number of carbon 14 determinations[5]. The two pottery types characteristic of this period are Galo Polychrome and Carrillo Polychrome. The former type comprises open or globular bowls, cylindrical vases with rectangular feet, anthropomorphic jars, and jars in the form of a human head *(Pl. 53)*; they are fashioned from finely textured clay and are painted in red and black on a light brown or orange slip, with a well burnished surface. The main subjects are highly stylised animals of angular outline—jaguars, snakes, monkeys or two-headed crocodiles *(Pl. 52, 54)*. They are painted in red and edged with a black line, or shown in silhouette on a black ground.

Carrillo Polychrome comprises rather crude vessels ranging in colour from buff to light brown, usually without a slip and with little if any burnishing. They are decorated with highly schematic and rapidly sketched designs, usually conventional representations of animals. The patches of red paint are invariably surrounded by a black line. The shapes include tripod bowls of simple form, big-bellied jars, sometimes anthropomorphic in form, and vases in the form of human heads.

The polychrome statuettes of this period possess the same technical qualities and are painted in the same style as the Galo vases *(Pl. 55)*. These figurines, which are hollow and range in size from 6 to over 30 cm., represent women in a standing position, or seated with their legs apart, sometimes with a child in their arms. Painting is used to give emphasis to elements represented in relief and to reproduce the details of clothing, tattooing and body painting.

Meanwhile pottery with bichrome decoration continues to be popular, using simple linear motifs painted in black or white on a red ground. There are also tripod vessels, sometimes with painted decoration, which are scored with an area of stippling or hatching on the bottom and were evidently used as graters; but these are confined to the northern part of the sector.

Apart from the pottery we know little about the phases of the Early Polychrome period. The sites seem to be more numerous than in the preceding period, and the shell-middens point to the importance of molluscs in the diet of the coastal peoples. At Papagayo (Bay of Culebra) a cemetery of secondary burials was excavated—shallow pits covered with large stones which were visible on the surface. Each pit contained the bones of from one to four persons, accompanied by pottery. The material recovered at other sites includes clay ear-spools and cylindrical seals and three-legged *metates* with bas-relief decoration.

As in the preceding period, it is difficult to relate the southern sector to any specific sphere of influence. The most representative types of Early

Polychrome pottery show borrowing from both the south and the north[6]. Lying at a distance from the great Maya centres, the southern sector assimilated influences from this source by an indirect route, through the cultures of Honduras and El Salvador. It seems also to have maintained its connections with southern Costa Rica and northern Panama.

Period IV

In this and the following period the northern sector is of more limited extent than in earlier periods. Northern Nicaragua and southern Honduras are detached from it and now form part of the southern sector. The boundary between the two sectors would thus pass to the west of the Gulf of Fonseca.

Northern Sector (950-1200 A.D.)

Having regard to the inadequacy of our evidence, Period IV in the northern sector can only be given the limiting dates of Early Post-Classic in the Maya area, the period following the collapse of the Classic civilisation.

In Honduras the beginning of the period is marked by the abandonment or decline of the great Classic centres. At Los Naranjos the only traces of occupation attributable to the Río Blanco phase are a few groups of mounds, including two ball courts, on the periphery of the area belonging to the Yojoa phase. Elsewhere Río Blanco sherds are extremely rare. In the Comayagua valley, Yarumela and Tenampua were finally abandoned; and the same fate overtook most of the numerous smaller sites like Lejamani or Lo de Vaca. We know of only three sites which were occupied in Period IV —Las Vegas, Quebrada de Arenal and another site near Quelepa[7]. In the Ulúa valley the only secure evidence comes from Santa Rita, where the first two levels in the stratigraphy contain sherds of X Fine Orange type, a horizon marker of Early Post-Classic[2].

Las Vegas consists of hut bases constructed of stones and earth, with an average diameter of 10 metres, and usually less than ½ metre in height. The pottery found here comprises a considerable proportion of monochrome types, sherds of imported Tohil Plumbate ware (another horizon marker of the Early Post-Classic), and the Las Vegas Polychrome type. This last type, with painted decoration in orange, red, brown and black on a cream slip, belongs to the Papagayo group of the southern sector. It is also found in the Río Blanco complex at Los Naranjos, accompanied by censers, either cylindrical or with handles (including one of "Mixtec" type). The ball courts with which this pottery is associated are constructed of earth and undressed limestone blocks; one of them is T-shaped, the other I-shaped.

In El Salvador, Tazumal still shows a certain amount of activity, at least during part of the period. This is the date assigned to the last building phase of Structure I, as well as to a number of new structures, meagre occupation levels containing Papagayo, Tohil Plumbate and some Mixtec incense-burners. Probably also to be dated to this period is the large stela said to have been found near the foot of the west side of Structure I, showing a standing figure with a head which is thought to represent Tlaloc *(Pl. 56)*.

Apart from Tazumal our only information on this period comes from various objects which were not recovered by scientifically conducted excavation but can nevertheless be securely dated to the period. In this category are the polychrome pottery of the Papagayo group *(Pl. 57, 59)* and the Plumbate vases *(Pl. 58)* to be found in so many collections. Tlaloc's face is depicted on Plumbate jars *(Pl. 62)*, as well as on small long-necked jugs *(Pl. 63)* and incense-burners. Some tripod plates and bowls, with feet in the form of animals' heads and decorative motifs (including the *joyel del viento*, the emblem of Quetzalcoatl in his manifestation as Ehecatl, the wind god) painted in red on buff, are very close to the bichrome vessels of the Tula-Mazapán horizon in Central Mexico *(Pl. 60, 61)*. A pottery

81   82

84

86   87

88

89

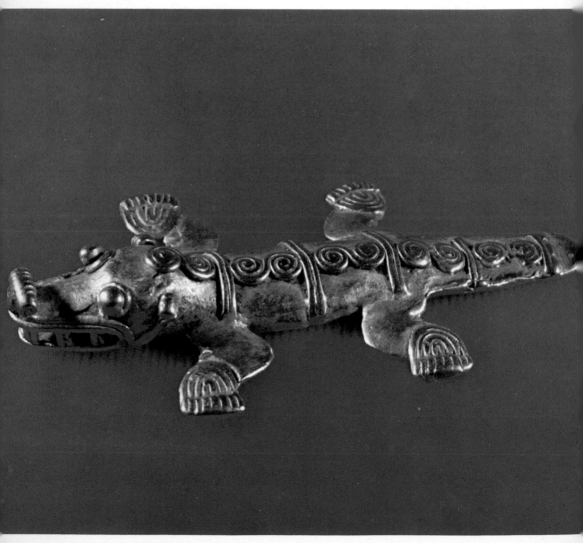

statue 1.40 metres high representing Xipe Totec, from the Chalchuapa region, is the replica of another figure found at Coatlinchan in the Valley of Mexico and also dated to the Mazapán horizon. The *chacmool* (a stone figure of a man lying on his back and holding an offering bowl) is another Toltec element which has been recognised in western Salvador.

All these features of Mexican origin probably stemmed from certain Nahua-speaking Pipil tribes whose descendants lived in western Salvador at the beginning of the 16th century. Cihuatán (Department of San Salvador) belongs—at least in part—to this period, to judge from the few fragments of pottery we have from this site. It comprises four large squares bounded by walls, several pyramidal structures and a ball court in the shape of a capital I. Structure I, which stands 18 metres high, has staircases with balustrades on three of its sides. It is built of blocks of dressed stone bound with mortar, with a facing of very hard plaster.

Pending the fuller information which excavation will bring, it seems reasonable to suppose that western Salvador enjoyed certain advantages over the rest of the northern sector. Mexican, and particularly Toltec, influences were dominant, and were reflected in a great variety of objects. There can be no doubt that the cultural level attained in this area was higher than in Honduras.

In Honduras the abandonment of the large centres at the very beginning of the period and the striking drop in population, as shown by the reduction in the number and size of the sites, evidently reflected a catastrophic situation. It seems reasonable to suppose that the Late Classic cultures of Honduras, living as they did in the shadow of Maya civilisation and sharing in that civilisation, though to a limited extent and on a limited scale, were unable to withstand the effects of the Maya collapse. The cultures which then took their place abandoned most of the older traditions, retaining only the ball game and some other features, and succumbed to the attraction of the new cultural focus in the south.

Southern Sector (800-1200 A.D.)

This sector is much larger than in earlier periods, and now comprises, in addition to north-western Costa Rica, the whole of the Pacific coast of Nicaragua—including the eastern shore of Lake Nicaragua—and of Honduras. Period IV appears to begin some 150 years earlier in this sector than in the northern sector[9]. The first feature of the period to be recorded is a striking increase in population, demonstrated throughout the sector by a rapid rise in the number and size of sites. In the coastal area of Costa Rica and particularly round the Bay of Culebra the Middle Polychrome occupation, marked by shell-middens and Papagayo sherds, is practically uninterrupted for a distance of many miles. During a reconnaissance in the Tempisque valley twelve out of 21 sites visited were found to be datable to this period in whole or in part; and similar observations were made by archaeologists working in Nicaragua, on the isthmus of Rivas and on the island of Ometepe. The sites are sometimes marked by mounds between 1 and 2 metres in height, which are only rarely laid out round open squares. At Papagayo (Bay of Culebra) there is a rectangular open space with waste heaps (fragments of pottery and sea shells) along the sides and large circular stone-lined houses at each end. At El Espino (Choluteca valley), in the northern part of the sector, two substructures of temples were found side by side on the same platform in the centre of the site. The rest of the site consists of house platforms, rarely more than a metre high, apparently laid out without any regular plan. On the shores of the Gulf of Fonseca are remains of seasonal encampments occupied by fishermen and shellfish gatherers, and also by salt-pan workers.

The polychrome pottery, which in the preceding period had been limited to a very small number of types, now developed in a remarkable way.

The unity of the southern sector was maintained by the distribution of types belonging to the Papagayo group (also known as Nicoya), which are characterised by orange, red and blackish-brown painting on a cream-coloured slip. The principal shapes are tripod plates and bowls with zoo-morphic or conical supports, pear-shaped jars and bowls with a pedestal base, vases and bowls in animal form (jaguars, coatis, turkeys) *(Pl. 64)*, and vases in the shape of a human head. Some of these forms reproduce those found in the Early Post-Classic pottery of Mesoamerica like Tohil Plumbate or X Fine Orange. The decoration consists of friezes made up either of purely geometric patterns or of conventional representations of mythological animals. The main theme is almost always provided by animals, the species most commonly found being snakes—usually in the form of the feathered serpent *(Pl. 65)*—jaguars and crocodiles. Human beings are rarely represented *(Pl. 67, 68)*. The grotesque faces found on certain vases may represent masks *(Pl. 66, 71)*. Within the Papagayo group we can observe differences between a northern and a southern area, which might be broadly defined by a line passing through Bagaces. To the north of the line, for example, we find as characteristic types vases decorated with large numbers of little jaguars or serpents' heads picked out in white against a black ground and bowls supported on three large serpents' heads modelled in high relief. Polychrome types other than those of the Papagayo group—e.g., Mora and Birmania—are rare or non-existent to the north of the line. The Mora type consists mainly of hemispherical bowls with decoration (almost always geometric) painted in red and black on light brown and orange grounds. The typical Birmania vessels are tripod bowls and zoomorphic vases with highly stylised animals painted in several colours on a light brown ground. Both of these types, which are abundant in the Tempisque valley, are found as imports in the Central Valley and in north-eastern and south-western Costa Rica. The ceramic complexes of the southern sector also include polychrome types of inferior quality, both technically and aesthetically, which continue Early Polychrome traditions, as well as pottery with incised decoration, which is geometric and rather crudely executed in the southern part of the sector, and figural and of high quality in the northern part.

The pottery of this period also includes the incense-burners with covers *(Pl. 73, 74)* which may have made their first appearance in an earlier period. These are hemispherical bowls on an annular base, with bell-shaped covers surmounted by figures of animals—jaguars, crocodiles (sometimes two-headed) or toads. They have an unslipped brown surface, decorated with areas of white-painted spikes.

We also find female figurines, cast in moulds and of hollow construction, showing the technical characteristics and the style of the Mora or Papagayo polychrome types. These vary considerably in size, and show the figure in a variety of attitudes—seated with legs apart or standing or kneeling *(Pl. 75)*. Animal statuettes are more rarely found: we may note, for instance, two standing figures of a jaguar and a female crocodile *(Pl. 76, 77)*.

The monumental sculpture of Nicaragua, which dates from this period and/or the following period[10], presents two different styles. The first is represented by statues found on the islands in Lake Nicaragua (Ometepe, Zapatera, Pensacola) and Lake Managua (Momotombito), and more rarely in the isthmus of Rivas, between the Pacific and the lakes. Although none of these have been recovered by scientific excavation, we know from evidence recorded more than a century ago that they were found associated with mounds[11].

Most of these statues—the lower part of which was left rough and buried in the ground—represent some form of association between a man and an animal. The man is shown life-size, seated on a bench or standing with his back against a support of some kind, and the animal—a crocodile or jaguar—is perched on his shoulders or clinging to his back *(Pl. 78, 79)*. Even more commonly, only the animal's head is shown, carried on the man's shoulders or on his head *(Pl. 83)*; in the latter case it may almost completely cover the man's head, like a helmet with the visor raised *(Pl. 81)*. The man's face thus appears to be caught in the animal's jaws, reproducing a theme frequently found in Mesoamerica. Sometimes his head disappears completely under the animal's face *(Pl. 82)*. The animals depicted in these sculptures include coyotes, snakes and vultures as well as crocodiles and jaguars. Other examples of sculpture include human figures seated on a high pedestal or a drum *(Pl. 80)*, animals seated on a bench, a man standing in a pose similar to the "sacrificers" of central Costa Rica, and a small rectangular stela with bas-relief figures of snakes on two of its sides.

The association between a man and an animal which is the commonest theme in this statuary is traditionally interpreted as the relationship between an individual and his *alter ego;* the animal on the man's head or shoulders is seen as his guardian spirit, his "individual totem". The statues may also be interpreted as representing divinities depicted in human form with an animal mask on their head, sometimes covering it completely: we have numerous examples of this in Mesoamerica, in particular the Zapotec urns and the Aztec divinities in the *Codex Borbonicus*. Again, the figures may be political or religious leaders, wearing a mask (a term to be understood in a wide sense, i.e., it may cover not only the head but the whole body) to indicate their title, their function, their membership of a particular clan, and so on.

The second type of sculpture is found to the east of Lake Nicaragua, in an area some 60 miles long and 30 miles across with the Department of Chontales in the centre. These statues—most of which are still unpublished —are cylindrical or prismatic columns, with a diameter of 50 cm. and a height of between 1 and 4.80 metres, on which a standing figure is carved in low relief. The head is slightly separated from the body, often by a shallow groove in the stone; the limbs are represented by long rectangular strips bent at right angles. The quality of these works varies widely, even within a single site: the figure may be roughly sketched in a few lines, or may be shown wearing clothing, weapons or ornaments. The clothing consists merely of belts or, more rarely, of loincloths, of which we possess one very elaborate example *(Pl. 84)*; the headdress is a turban, sometimes with a small animal perched on top *(Pl. 86)*. Many of the figures are shown wearing a necklace and pectoral, the form of which is reminiscent of the gold "eagles" of Panama and Costa Rica *(Pl. 85)*. Others are shown holding a lance *(Pl. 87)*. On the largest of these statues, which come from San Pedro de Lóvago, there are some small silhouettes of monkeys round the main figure *(Pl. 88)*. One of the sculptures from El Salto shows a figure seated on a pedestal wearing a mask, so far unidentified; and the same mask is found on the head of one of the figures from San Pedro de Lóvago *(Pl. 89)*. This figure may represent a divinity; the others seem to be local chieftains.

The origins of the Chontales style, like those of the sculpture found on the islands, are still obscure. The practice of representing a man or animal in bas-relief on a column is common in Central America and elsewhere: examples are known in El Salvador, Guatemala, Honduras (Ulúa valley), southern Costa Rica and Panama, and as far away as Colombia and Peru. In general, however, these works are cruder and of smaller size than the Chontales statues. The Chontales figures have only a few features in common with the statues found on the islands in the lakes—the figure seated on a pedestal, the animals on the headdress and certain decorative motifs like interlocking figures-of-eight or crosses. In both cases the sculpture seems to represent a distinctive local development of uncertain filiation. Some of its features are found in the south, like the miniature animal on the headdress or the figure of the "sacrificer"; others are more clearly Meso-american, like the human head within an animal's jaws, the slit drum and the rectangular stela with representations of snakes.

In brief, the southern sector reached its apogee in Period IV. The sites increased in number and in size; the range of stone implements was extended, and the bow and arrow became part of the equipment of the hunter and the warrior; and the craftsmen of the period, while maintaining earlier traditions (the three-legged *metates* with carved decoration and the jadeite ornaments), reached out into new fields (monumental sculpture and gold jewellery). Although the Conquistadors extracted from the native population such impressive quantities of ornaments of gold and *tumbaga* (an alloy of gold and copper, with silver present as an impurity), articles of this kind are very rarely found in tombs: evidently it was not the general custom to deposit gold objects with the dead. The ornaments, which were probably imported, reproduce forms which originated in Panama or Costa Rica *(Pl. 90)*. The pottery, often of high quality, is very varied, but we also find certain types of decoration (particularly in Mora and Birmania) reproduced in exact detail in thousands of copies. It seems likely that there were workshops specialising in the production of particular types or varieties. The network of trading contacts extended southward as far as the Central Valley and Diquís delta in Costa Rica. Thus for the first time the cultures of the southern sector found themselves firmly within the Mesoamerican sphere of influence.

According to a Nicarao tradition recorded in the 17th century by the historian Torquemada, the Nicarao and Chorotega peoples originally lived in the Soconusco area (Chiapas), but were forced to leave it because of the harrying they suffered from their neighbours. The Chorotega, who were the first to leave, found a new home on the Pacific coast of Nicaragua and the Guanacaste area. Later came the Nicarao, who drove the Chorotega out of the isthmus of Rivas and into the neighbouring areas, particularly the Nicoya peninsula. From the details given in this account it has been estimated that the two peoples left Soconusco about 800 A.D.; and since this date corresponds with the beginning of Period IV in this sector it

seems very likely that the cultural development we have observed was due
to the arrival of the Chorotega in Nicaragua.

Period V (1200-1525)

This period corresponds to the Late Post-Classic or Protohistoric period
in Mesoamerican chronology. Our documentation is extremely uneven:
we know practically nothing about this period in the northern sector,
but in the southern sector the Late Polychrome of Nicaragua and Costa
Rica is known from a number of sites.

Northern Sector

The few pages devoted to the site of Naco (northern Honduras) in the
report by Strong, Kidder and Paul are our only source of information.
At the time of Cortés's expedition to Honduras in 1525 Naco was a town
of some 10,000 inhabitants. The central area where Strong and his associates
conducted their investigations comprises a masonry pyramid 4 metres
high, a square surrounded by house platforms, and a ball court. This
seems, like most of the earlier examples, to have been I-shaped; and, like
the courts of Post-Classic Mexico, it has two stone rings through which
the players sought to put the ball. The floors and walls of the
houses were covered with a coating of stucco painted in bright
colours. Naco Polychrome, the most characteristic pottery type, comprises
tripod bowls painted in red and black on a cream ground. The motifs
are mainly geometric, and the work is rather carelessly done. There are
also some pieces of stamped pottery, others bearing the impression of
fabrics, and a few sherds of European origin.

The Mexican influences (masonry construction, the use of stucco, the
rings used in the ball game) are no doubt the result of the movement of
Nahuatl settlers into the area. It is significant that the Nahuatl language
is believed to have been spoken in this area.

94

99

100

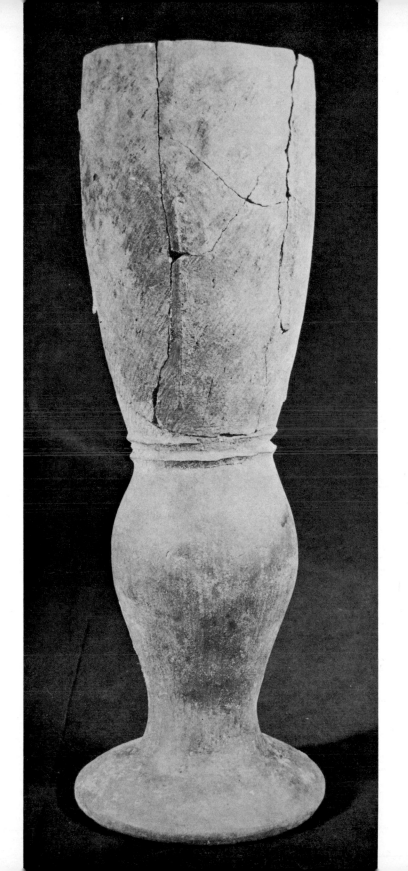

102

103

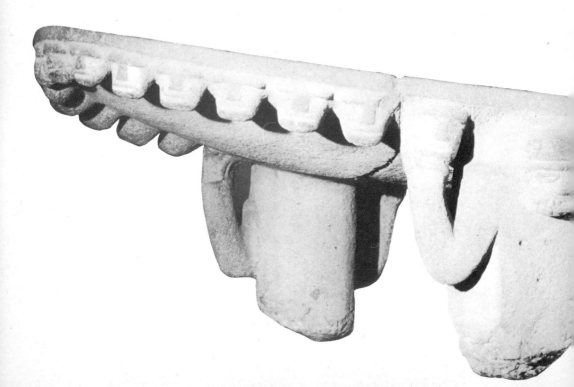

104

105

106

107

108

Southern Sector

In this sector the period can be divided into two parts. The first part [12] sees the appearance of new polychrome types (Vallejo, Jicote, Mombacho) belonging to the Papagayo group, which show more marked and more direct Mexican influence than in the preceding period *(Pl. 92, 93, 96-98)*. Certain vases bear figures which can be recognised as representations of divinities like Ehecatl and the Earth Monster *(Pl. 97)*. In the second part of the period, which begins shortly before the Conquest and continues after it, differences can be observed between the areas to the north and south of a line drawn through Bagaces. North of this line, Luna Polychrome almost entirely eclipses the earlier types of painted pottery. The shapes are much the same as before—mainly tripod bowls with feet in the form of serpents' or crocodiles' heads—but the style of painting is radically different from the Papagayo manner: the representations of animals have now become purely conventional, and are sketched in with tenuous black lines, which are frequently barbed and picked out with patches of colour. This type continued in use until the Conquest, for examples have been found in association with European iron. South of the line through Bagaces, Luna ware is very rare, and is probably imported. The decoration on pottery consists almost solely of incision and modelling, and painted decoration disappears altogether. This is confirmed by the fact that the chroniclers make no reference to painted pottery: Oviedo was delighted by the pottery vessels on the island of Chira (Gulf of Nicoya), which he described as being of a lustrous black and declared were fit to grace a prince's table. He was no doubt referring to pieces of Murrillo and Castillo type *(Pl. 94-95)*, which enjoyed great popularity—the former throughout the whole sector, the latter only in the northern part.

In the area round the Gulf of Fonseca (Honduras) we observe a similar displacement of polychrome decoration by relief decoration in a variety of techniques—appliqué, modelling, incision, zoned reed-impressions, etc. Catracho Polychrome, which had first appeared during the preceding phase, with its decoration of linear geometric patterns in black and red on a buff ground, is somewhat reminiscent of the rather clumsy style of Naco Polychrome.

It is probable that the changes which took place in the pottery in the 13th century, showing strong Mexican influence, were introduced by the Nicarao people, though our information is still so incomplete that we are unable to assert this positively. On the other hand certain features of the Post-Classic cultures of the southern sector are very probably of southern origin: e. g., the communal circular houses of Papagayo, which have no counterpart in the north but are recorded at Orosí (Cartago valley) in the Chibcha zone. Again, from a burial on the same site, we have bracelets of human teeth accompanied by Luna and Murrillo pottery: these have not been recorded in the north, but we have examples from Panama (Herrera phase of Parita) and Colombia (Tairona). Thus even in a period which seems to be one of total Mesoamerican dominance the southern sector plays the part of a "frontier" in which exchanges and borrowings take place between many different areas.

Zone of South American Tradition

This zone extends from the north coast of Honduras to the Colombian frontier, taking in most of Honduras and Nicaragua, almost the whole of Costa Rica (excluding only the present-day province of Guanacaste) and Panama. Most of the archaeological work in this zone has been concentrated on the southern half of the zone, but even this area is very imperfectly known. Certain periods are relatively well documented, while others show a complete blank in the chronological charts.

Period I (?–2100 B.C.)

The history of the zone begins with the two fluted points found on the surface at Madden Lake (Panama Canal), which show a fairly close resemblance to the specimens from Guanacaste discovered in the collection purchased by Hartman.

Five or six millennia later a small group of fishermen and shellfish gatherers left traces of occupation on the site of Cerro Mangote (Parita Bay, Panama). They were ignorant of the use of pottery and probably also of agriculture, and their equipment was confined to a few simple querns, pebbles used as grinding or crushing tools, and unretouched flakes. Bone awls and shell beads have also been found. The burials are of two kinds, primary (with the body in a flexed position) and secondary (the bones being gathered together and buried in a bundle). Cerro Mangote has been given a carbon 14 dating of 4850 ± 100 B.C.

Period II (2100–300 B.C.)

The period begin at the site of Monagrillo (Parita Bay) with the phase of that name. The ceramic complex, dated to 2130 B.C., is the oldest known in the isthmus. Some recent discoveries appear to indicate that pottery appeared much earlier in South America than in Mesoamerica. The oldest ceramic complexes known are those found in Ecuador and Colombia: at Puerto Hormiga, on the Caribbean coast of Colombia, the pottery is dated to 4875 ± 170 B.C. It is thus highly probable that the pottery of Monagrillo is of southern origin. Of limited typology and rather crude workmanship, it is sometimes decorated with incised curvilinear motifs or bands of red paint on a buff ground. Like the people of Cerro Mangote, the occupants of the Monagrillo site lived on fish and shellfish, together with wild plants and berries. Agriculture, if practised at all, does not seem to have played a large part in their lives. The stone implements include *metates* and mortars, beaters, pestles, rectangular *manos* (hand-stones used on a *metate*) and flake tools, better prepared than at Cerro Mangote.

At Monagrillo another ceramic complex known as Sarigua has been identified. This is notable for its decorative techniques—incision, shell stamping, puctation and appliqué fillets. The excavators of the site dated it hypothetically, basing themselves on typological criteria, to the beginning of the first millennium, although other authorities believe that it may well be much later. But whatever the correct date of the Sarigua complex may be, the sequence shows a blank extending over several centuries, for it is only at the beginning of Period III that we are able to resume contact with the archaeology of the zone.

Periods III (300 B.C. to 300 A.D.) and IV (300–500 A.D.)

Period III is so far represented only in Panama and southern Costa Rica. It is identified by the wide distribution of two pottery types, Scarified and Guacamayo. The distinctive decoration of Scarified consists of an alternation of groups of incised lines and patches of colour, usually red *(Pl. 101)*. This technique is very close to the Zoned Bichrome style of Costa Rica and Nicaragua (particularly in the Bocana type), found in pottery dated between 300 B.C. and 300 A.D. Scarified pottery is found from southern Costa Rica to the province of Coclé, taking in on the way the provinces of Chiriquí and Veraguas. The Guacamayo type is represented by tall narrow vases of complex profile with a decoration consisting of parallel incised lines, brush strokes, appliqué fillets, and sometimes a band of red paint *(Pl. 102)*. Pottery of this type has been recorded in the Azuero peninsula as far as Tonosí, in Coclé and Veraguas; it seems to be rare, or entirely absent, in Chiriquí.

Barriles (Chiriquí) has not yet received the archaeological attention it deserves. Its very distinctive sculpture is notable particularly for the life-size statues depicting a man, naked and without any ornaments, carrying on his shoulders a figure wearing a conical hat and an ornament round his neck *(Pl. 104)*. These strange couples (victor and vanquished, or master and slave) stand on a slender pedestal which enables the statues to be set into the ground. There are also figures of a man standing with his hands hanging by his sides or in the attitude of the "beheader" or "sacrificer"—a type which is found, scarcely modified, in central Costa Rica until shortly before the Conquest: the man holds a severed head at arm's length in his right hand and brandishes an axe in his left *(Pl. 105)*. The large round or oval tables with a continuous line of human heads round the edge, found in Panama and Costa Rica in later periods, are already represented at Barriles *(Pl. 106)*. The pottery provides examples of themes which persist throughout the centuries *(cf. Pl. 103 and 120)*. It includes vases with Zoned Bichrome decoration *(Pl. 108)*, and others with relief figures of animals on the rim or the body. According to Stirling [13] there are also tripod vessels painted in two colours (red and yellow) and vases with negative painting (the "lost-colour" technique). The tombs consist of a burial chamber, 2 metres in diameter, and an entrance shaft; the use of funerary urns, with an upturned bowl as a lid, seems to be general. The offerings consist of three- or four-legged *metates*, often of considerable size. No mounds have been recorded, but there are "rectangular floors or foundations of massive stone slabs and boulders".

Barriles is a site of astonishing maturity for such an early period. Before its discovery the level of civilisation in Chiriquí in this period was thought to be no more than a group of unpretentious village communities: the picture as we now see it is very different. We may recall in this connection the example of Guanacaste, where the cemeteries of Las Huacas and Bolson, if considered in isolation, give a quite inadequate impression of the culture of their period.

The Santa María complex from the site of Girón (Parita) is dated between 300 and 500 A.D. (Period IV). Pottery from other areas can also be assigned to this period on the basis of its analogies with elements in the Santa María and Ciruelas (Guanacaste) complexes[14].

Period V (500-800 A.D.)

On the evidence of the pottery, in which the design is painted in red and outlined in black against a light brown ground, most of the tombs at Venado Beach belong to this period. The interest of this cemetery lies in the great variety of burial types which it offers. The bodies are buried in urns, or in a seated position, or recumbent (either extended or flexed). The cemetery also provides evidence of a custom which is found at Sitio Conte and is recorded by the Spanish chroniclers—the practice of killing the dead man's servants and burying them along with him. Other skeletons found here in a mutilated or disarticulated form are probably the remains of sacrificial victims. The Venado Beach cemetery provides evidence of a hierarchical society in which an elite (whether political or military or religious, or all three at once) wielded sufficient power over their subjects or slaves to persuade them—or force them—to accompany their masters into the tomb. Some burials contain gold ornaments, which, along with the material found in the oldest tombs at Sitio Conte (Coclé) are the earliest evidence yet available for the appearance of metal-working in Central America.

Some of the burials at Sitio Conte are dated to this period by pottery of Early Coclé style *(Pl. 111)*. With it there are sometimes associated pendants of bone or marine ivory, or of semi-precious stones like agate or serpentine.

Central and eastern Costa Rica finally enter the sequence with the Curridabat complex[15], established by Hartman in the cemetery of that name near San José. This includes large tripod vases with long hollow rattle feet decorated with relief figures of animals—mostly crocodiles, but also snakes, toucans and other birds. More elaborate designs are also found, for example a man wearing a bird mask, or vultures devouring human bodies *(Pl. 115)*. Appliqué decoration is also very characteristic of this complex, and decorations consisting of rows of appliqué pellets are found on globular pots, hemispherical bowls and squat jars *(Pl. 114)*. Finally Hartman records some small jars with negative painting in red on black. In addition to the pottery the Curridabat burials—which, unlike those of the following period, are simple pits with no surface indication—contained axes of polished stone and mace-heads similar to those found in Guanacaste.

North-eastern Honduras (the Caribbean coast and Bay Islands) is represented in this period by the Selin phase (Epstein, 1956). Its pottery shows a blending of two traditions of different origins. The Manatee type (also known as North Coast Appliqué) with appliqué and incised decoration, belongs to the Caribbean tradition, which is much more interested in relief decoration than in painting. The San Marcos Polychrome type, on the other hand, shows influences derived from the painted pottery of Ulúa-Yojoa types. The objects other than pottery found by Strong—jade ornaments, three-legged *metates*, mace-heads, etc.—cannot be precisely dated; but some of them may belong to this period, giving evidence of close relationships with Costa Rica.

Period VI (800-1525 A.D.)

During this period the cultures of Panama and Costa Rica—like those of Colombia and the southern sector of the other zone—reached their apogee. The period is marked by a rapid increase in the number of sites and by a spectacular development of craft production, particularly of pottery, jewellery and stone sculpture.

The cemetery of Sitio Conte, in Panama, consists of rectangular pits containing anything from one to twelve bodies buried together; in several cases the burial is clearly that of a chief and his retinue. The richness of the tombs may indicate that, as in Darien in the 16th century (according to Oviedo), only the nobles and their dependants—wives, servants and slaves—were granted burial; the bodies of ordinary people were left to be devoured by wild animals and vultures. The Coclé Polychrome pottery (black, brown, dark red, light red, purple and sometimes green on a cream ground) has figures of animals, often "humanised" or hybrid and always highly stylised *(Pl. 119)*, forming rigorously symmetrical patterns made up of curvilinear elements. The double scroll plays an important part, both as an independent decorative feature and as a principle determining the arrangement of other motifs. The principal shapes are large round dishes, sometimes with a pedestal base, carafes and long-necked jars.

In the Parita Bay region two different styles of polychrome pottery have been identified in this period. The earlier of the two is curvilinear and shows close affinities with the Sitio Conte pottery. The patterns are often contained within rectangular and triangular panels, and are painted in black, red and/or purple on a cream, orange or reddish-brown ground *(Pl. 116, 117)*. Among animal representations the favourite subjects are the crocodile (shown in humanised form, standing or "dancing"—*Pl. 118*), fishes (hammerhead shark—*Pl. 120*—and ray) and birds. The commonest shapes are dishes on high pedestal bases and short-necked jars.

The second style, Hatillo, shows a greater variety of shapes, especially in the case of bottles. The decoration is made up of rectilinear and angular elements in red outlined in black, using Greek key patterns in place of scrolls. The representations have a schematic air and have lost something of their earlier elegance.

The jewellery and gold ornements of Coclé are known to us in detail from Lothrop's excavations at Sitio Conte. This work shows such remarkable

112

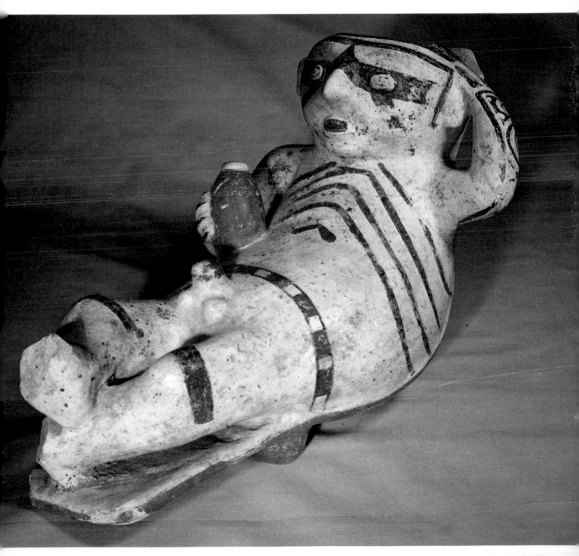

117→

116

119

121

122

126

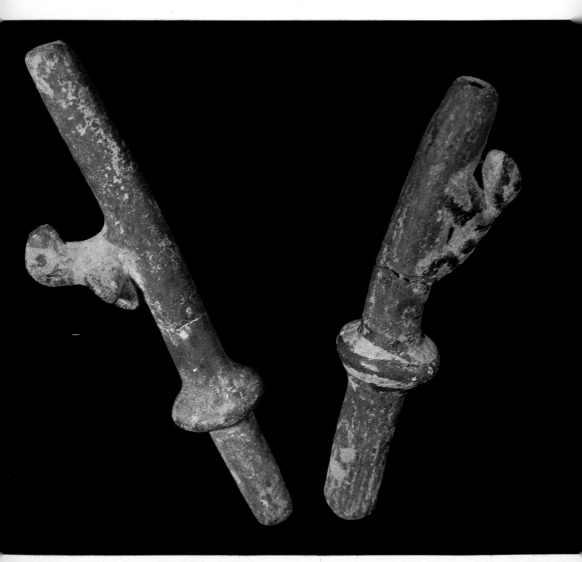

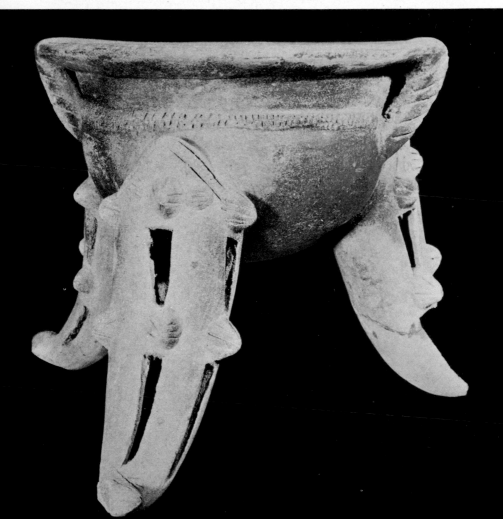

variety—in the use of materials, shapes and techniques—that the summary account given here cannot hope to do it full justice.

Gold foil was wrought by cold hammering into head-bands, helmets, bracelets, beads, nose and ear ornaments, and large circular pectoral plaques with repoussé decoration *(Pl. 122)*. It was also used to cover ornaments made of whale-tooth ivory, pottery, resin or wood. Pendants were cast from gold or *tumbaga* in the shape of human and animal figurines; the animals represented include crocodiles, monkeys or dogs with curling tails, monkeys standing erect, and birds. These works are hollow, being cast by the *cire perdue* process round a core of clay and charcoal. The gilding of the *tumbaga* pieces was carried out by the process known as *mise en couleur*, in which the copper in the alloy on the outside of the object was eaten away by vegetable acids so that only the gold was left on the surface. Separate pieces could be welded together by melting or hammering, and there are also examples of pieces joined by soldering (using a solder with a lower melting point than the two parts to be assembled). Other ornaments were made of agate, serpentine, whale-tooth ivory, sharks' or dogs' teeth, peccary tusks, etc. *(Pl. 121)*.

In the jewellery of Veraguas the figurines cast in *tumbaga* or gold are technically less complex than the corresponding objects of Coclé type, being "open-backed". They include many representations of animals—particularly "eagles" (in reality vultures) and frogs, but also jaguars, dogs, sharks, turtles, etc. The animals are frequently humanised, the head being animal but the body and attitude human. Features characteristic of several different animals can also be combined in a single creature: an "eagle", for example, has its head flanked by two pairs of crocodile heads, and wears a jaguar's head on its body.

In addition to gold ornaments the tombs of Veraguas (which are of the shaft-and-chamber type) contain large and elegant *metates* in the form of a jaguar, with an oval top borne on four legs in which the animal's head projects in front and its tail is joined to one of its legs. The rim and the jaguar have a guilloche ornament in bas-relief. This type of *metate* is also found, with some variants, in Chiriquí and central Costa Rica. Three-legged tables with a carved panel on the underside are common. The pottery includes polychrome ware which is thought to be imported from Coclé or the Azuero peninsula, as well as local types, mostly monochrome, in unusual shapes—bottles with tall elongated necks, flat-bottomed jars which appear to be cut in half, tripod vases with looped supports, etc.

The pottery of Chiriquí and southern Costa Rica shows some original styles not found elsewhere in Panama. In the unpainted ware a characteristic form is a tall tripod with hollow feet; some of these are similar to the Curridabat tripods of Costa Rica and may well be contemporary with them. The vase, which has a pointed base, is decorated with a ridge running round the upper part, and on the top of the feet are modelled figures of small animals *(Pl. 135)*. The other tripod vessels are hemispherical bowls with appliqué and punctated ornament and two twisted handles, borne on feet in the form of animals (usually fish—*Pl. 134*) or human beings. The bowl shown in *Plate 137* is supported by three female figures, each suffering from a different complaint (one in the head, the second in the abdomen, the third in the breast).

Another type which is well represented is a buff ware, thin-walled with a rough surface texture, the commonest shapes being short-necked jars with rounded or pointed bases and small tripod bowls. The decoration is confined to small appliqué pellets and fillets on the neck and two modelled figures of animals (armadillos, monkeys or frogs), often of very small size, one on either side *(Pl. 136)*. The purity of line and restraint of the decoration is unusual in Central America. This type also has miniature imitations of basalt stools, the round seat being borne by Atlas figures. The one shown in *Plate 133* also reproduces the form of a metal pendant depicting

194

a hybrid creature, with the body and posture of a human being, the wings of an "eagle" and the head of a jaguar.

After so much inventiveness and ingenuity it is disappointing to turn to the painted pottery (red and black on a light brown ground) of Chiriquí. This can be divided into three broad groups. The first is decorated with stylised animals (crocodiles) in the technique already familiar to the reader, with areas of red colouring surrounded by black lines *(Pl. 126)*; in the second the patterns are purely conventional or geometric, based on the use of triangles and dots; and the third uses geometric ornament painted in negative technique *(Pl. 125)*. A more imaginative approach is found in the ocarinas, whistles and figurines painted in the same style as the second group, with figures of jaguars, armadillos, crocodiles *(Pl. 128)*, tapirs and birds *(Pl. 127)*, as well as human beings in a variety of attitudes —men and women standing or sitting, women with a child at the breast *(Pl. 124)*, grinding corn with the *metate*, gossiping or hunting vermin.

Although gold objects from Chiriquí have been available in European and American collections for more than a century, they have not yet been the subject of systematic study. The figurines are either completely hollow and cast over a core, as at Coclé, or "open-backed". The usual animals are found ("eagles", jaguars, fishes, etc.), together with some original features—for example the pendants in which the main subject is enclosed within a frame. These pieces often have bangles attached. In the jewellery of the Diquís delta *(Pl. 130, 131)* we can recognise strong influences from other areas, particularly from Veraguas but also from Chiriquí—"eagles" holding a tiny animal or man in their beaks, standing figures *(Pl. 132)*, frogs with a pattern of filigree spirals round their mouths, and many other themes.

One feature common to Chiriquí and southern Costa Rica is the *metate* in the form of a jaguar, with four legs and an oval or rectangular top, which differs from the Veraguas type in being smaller or squatter. With some exceptions the sculpture of Chiriquí (in the Bugavita style) is rather crudely executed; in the Diquís area, on the other hand, the art of small-scale statuary is well developed. It includes pieces of flat sculpture in soft sandstone, rarely more than 50 cm. high, representing standing figures with a human or jaguar head *(Pl. 140, 141)*. In these the arms are marked off from the trunk by two rectangular slits, and a third slit similarly marks off the legs. We find other figures, along with animals (armadillos or jaguars) carved in low relief on a cylindrical piece of stone *(Pl. 139)*; and there are also small jaguars with disproportionately large heads depicted in a more realistic pose *(Pl. 138)*. Mention must also be made of the curious stone spheres, of geometrically perfect shape, which usually range between 1.20 and 1.50 metres in diameter but may be as much as 2 metres or more. They are sometimes found resting on foundations of pebbles designed to secure stability. Sometimes they are aligned in rows, and it has been suggested that in such cases their function may have been to mark a direction of astronomical significance. Elsewhere four spheres are thought to mark the four corners of a cemetery.

The archaeology of central, eastern and north-eastern Costa Rica is mainly known through the large quantity of material brought to light by *huaqueros*. The information obtainable from these clandestine diggers—though "clandestine" is only a relative term—is rarely reliable, and Hartman's work is still our only real source of information. It has been possible to date some of the objects discovered by him, both pottery and stone, on the basis of associations with the polychrome pottery of Guanacaste; but the chronological (even more than the geographical) placing of much of the material is still uncertain. Most of the objects appear to be "late", dating from shortly before the Conquest; but when they first occurred, and whether and in what direction they developed, are questions to which we can give no answer.

We shall consider together the Central Valley, the Reventazón valley, the Linea Vieja region (named after a railway line from Siquírres to Guápiles) and the San Carlos plain, although some variations between the different areas have been observed.

In the cemetery of Chircot (Cartago valley) Hartman excavated 205 tombs. These were pits paved with slabs of stone, and the grave goods accompanying the skeletons included sculpture and pottery. The pottery consisted of squat jars and tripod bowls, mostly with appliqué and incised decoration *(Pl. 142)* and sometimes with bichrome patterns of simple linear elements painted in white or yellow on a red ground. There was also polychrome ware of Mora and Birmania type, imported from Guanacaste.

At Orosí, in the same area, Hartman excavated 65 tombs, on two different levels, under the floors of large circular houses. In one of the 49 burials on the upper level were *millefiori* glass beads, dating it to after the Conquest. A single polychrome bowl of Birmania type was found in a tomb on the lower level. It is thus probable that most of the Orosí pottery is later than that found at Chircot—in particular the jars with composite-silhouette necks, the bottles of undulating outline, and the brown cylindrical vases with three feet in the form of snakes' heads, decorated with incised or relief ornament. Some tall tripod vessels found in the Linea Vieja area are manifestly imitations of the corresponding pieces from Diquís and Chiriquí *(Pl. 143)*. A number of other objects, usually unpainted, have been recorded in these various areas, but their dating is uncertain; they include figurines *(Pl. 145)*, whistles, ocarinas and *maracas* (rattles).

We have examples of basalt statuary from both Chircot and Orosí. These works are of small size (rarely more than 60 cm. high) and show only a limited range of subjects—though an effect of variety is obtained even within this restricted repertoire from the influence of local styles and the personality of the artist. There is a whole group of works depicting human sacrifice by beheading, with the "sacrificers" (whom we have already encountered at Barriles) brandishing an axe in one hand and a severed head in the other; sometimes, curiously, the "sacrificer" is a child *(Pl. 144)*. There are also standing figures with a head dangling from a rope *(Pl. 146, 147)*; prisoners and/or sacrificial victims with their hands tied behind their backs or above their heads *(Pl. 148)*; and severed heads, ranging from 15 to 20 cm. in height. The severed heads are sometimes also found in clay.

Other works of sculpture are clearly on religious or magical themes—standing figures wearing a crocodile mask and a double crown of feathers *(Pl. 149)* and shamans or medicine-men sitting in a crouching position and smoking a cigar, the smoke from which would be blown over the patient *(Pl. 150)*. There are also a number of statues of men and women in an erect position, naked and with no other distinctive sign than a cap: the women are shown holding their breasts in their hands. The legs are separated from the body, but the arms are usually joined to it.

The skill and imagination of the sculptors finds full play in a series of cult accessories—tables, stools and *metates* of all kinds. The *metates*, like those of Chiriquí, are in the form of jaguars, and sometimes also have Atlas figures (monkeys or small jaguars) between the legs *(Pl. 152)*. Some tables from the Linea Vieja region are closely imitated from the three-legged tables, with carving on the underside and a painted decoration of white lines *(Pl. 151)*. Certain tables or "altars" from the Reventazón valley are technical *tours de force:* cut from a single piece of stone and standing almost a metre high on their three feet, they have on the underside and between the feet a variety of scenes carved in high relief, of sufficient complexity to suggest that they depict incidents from some myth *(Pl. 153)*. There are also circular tables with an openwork pedestal base and a decoration of severed human or animal heads round the rim, stools supported by Atlas figures of monkeys or jaguars, miniature *metates*, and a variety of other items.

The Linea Vieja region—and more particularly the neighbourhood of Guápiles—is famous for its jadeite ornaments, of which thousands of examples are known *(Pl. 26, 154)*. These include, for example, necklaces containing hundreds of beads in the form of very thin discs. There are pendants similar to those of Guanacaste (axe-shaped ornaments with a bird's face, and tubular "beads" which may be as much as 35 cm. long), but there are many others of quite individual quality—human figures or humanised animals seen in profile, two-headed serpents and crocodiles, pendants in the form of outspread wings ("winged pendants"), etc. Certain forms are imitated from jewellery—frogs, "eagles", animals with curling tails (as at Coclé) and birds with long beaks *(Pl. 156)*. Some pieces have an openwork pattern obtained by the use of a special technique: a hole was made in the stone, and through this was passed a string, which with the help of an abrasive and water could be used as a saw *(Pl. 155)*. Maceheads are also found in the Linea Vieja region, and these, like the jadeite pendants, show greater variety of form and subject than in Guanacaste; they represent birds, jaguars' and crocodiles' heads, and also human heads *(Pl. 157–158)*.

Objects made of gold and *tumbaga* are very rare in the Central Valley, but are frequently found in eastern Costa Rica, in the Reventazón valley and at Guápiles *(Pl. 159, 160)*. The main subjects are "eagles" (often two-headed), but frogs and human figures are also found. Although mostly produced locally, the jewellery of Linea Vieja is closely imitated from models in Panama, particularly Coclé and Veraguas. Unexpectedly, too, we find figurines in the various styles of Colombia—Tairona, Quimbaya and Sinú.

In almost every case we can trace the origin of the work produced in central and eastern Costa Rica. The jewellery imitates the subjects and techniques of Coclé and Veraguas. The sculpture finds its inspiration in Veraguas (three-legged tables with a flying panel on the underside) and Chiriquí tables with a decoration of human heads round the rim, and the theme of the "sacrificer" at Barriles; later and in other areas, the stool with Atlas figures of jaguars, the circular tables on a pedestal base, the *metates* in the form of jaguars). The jadeite pendants and mace-heads find their models in Guanacaste, at any rate if it is accepted—and this has still to be proved—that the art of working jadeite did not appear in the Linea Vieja region until the beginning of our era. The pottery is in the Caribbean tradition of relief decoration, and borrows certain features from the Diquís and Chiriquí area (tripods) and Guanacaste (tripod feet in the form of serpents' heads in high relief, similar to those found in Luna Polychrome).

These close relations with other areas and regions have suggested to some scholars that Linea Vieja was an area of trade and interchange. This explanation does not seem adequate to account for the scale of the phenomenon. It seems more likely that, for reasons which are unknown because of the insufficiency of our documentation, central and particularly eastern Costa Rica was an area of convergence of a variety of influences, from which the local cultures were able to profit. No doubt as a result of the multiplicity of borrowings from different areas the "pupil" cultures were often able to surpass the work of their masters, particularly in the fields of sculpture and jewellery.

Equally striking is the contrast between the high standards of craftsmanship attained in so many fields (including woodworking, as we know from the miraculous discovery at Retes of wooden objects dated by carbon 14 analysis to 900 A.D.) and the total absence of architecture. Here and there on the Atlantic side of the isthmus there are mounds of earth covered with pebbles, which are sometimes of some length as if representing enclosure walls; and we have already noted the large circular houses of Orosí, similar to those found at Papagayo. We know also that the tombs are sometimes paved with slabs of stone and/or pebbles. But in terms of building technique

146

147

148

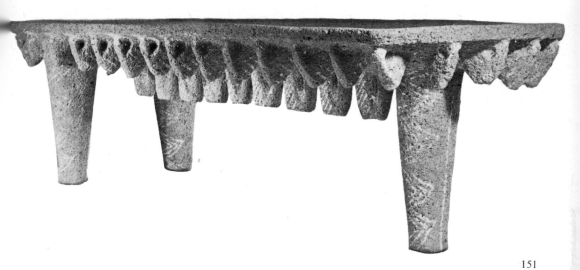

151

152

153

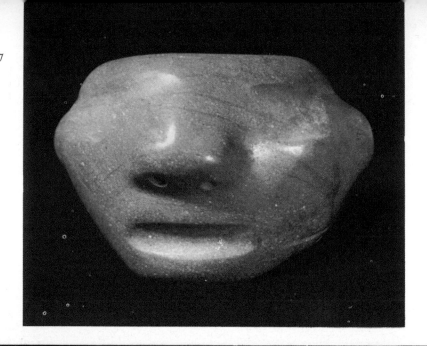

157

158

these are modest achievements indeed, showing no sign of the energy and skill displayed by the sculptors, the jewellers and the goldsmiths.

If we leave Costa Rica and turn northward we pass through immense areas of whose past we know nothing. It is not until we reach the northern coast of Honduras and the Bay Islands that we resume contact with the archaeological record. The pottery of the Cocal phase, which corresponds to the first part of this period, comprises on the one hand vessels with relief decoration which sometimes show close affinities with the pottery of central Costa Rica, and on the other a type with polychrome painting on a cream-coloured slip which may be modelled on pottery of the Papagayo group. Sherds of Plumbate ware and small copper bells have also been recorded. Later the Bay Island Polychrome disappears. Situated as it is on the boundary between the two zones, this region shows evidence of borrowings from both.

SUMMARY AND CONCLUSIONS

VI

Zone of Mesoamerican Tradition

Northern Sector

By 500 B.C.—if we can generalise from the Los Naranjos evidence—El Salvador and western Honduras were inhabited by peoples who had already attained a high cultural level, evidently as a result of the developments in Mesoamerica during the Middle Pre-Classic period. There is some indication that the Olmecs may have played a direct part in the formation of these cultures.

Two centuries before our era the particularism reflected in the pottery had given place to a greater degree of unity, as indicated by the extreme popularity of pottery with Usulután decoration throughout the whole sector, the building of pyramids and ceremonial centres, the use of figurines and incense-burners, and so on. The pottery—at least during the Early Classic period—was still sheltered from Maya influences, and went on tirelessly reproducing styles which had long fallen out of favour farther to the north.

From 550 to 950 A.D. the sector lived under the shadow of Maya civilisation and benefited from its example; but in spite of some striking achievements the cultures of Honduras and El Salvador had something of the status of poor relations compared with their brilliant neighbours. When the Maya civilisation fell, the dependent cultures soon followed suit. In Honduras the survivors seem then to have turned towards the new focal point in the south. Groups of Mexican origin—first the Nahua people in El Salvador, and later the Nahuatl throughout the whole of the sector—brought a little life to areas which had been unable to recover from the after-effects of the collapse of Maya civilisation.

Southern Sector

By the beginning of our era the cultures on the Pacific side of Costa Rica and Nicaragua already possessed most of the elements which they were to preserve throughout the whole of their history in pre-Columbian times —agriculture, pottery, three-legged decorated *metates*, jadeite ornaments. During the closing stages of the Pre-Classic and the whole of the Classic period this sector was a "frontier" (in the American sense of the term) in which autonomous cultures developed with the help of borrowings from the north, the east or the south.

The situation changed radically in the 9th century. With the arrival of the Chorotega, followed later by the Nicarao, the sector entered a period of prosperity which was reflected in a substantial increase in population, the development of craft production, the creation of distinctive styles in pottery and sculpture, and the extension of trading connections and cultural interchanges with other countries.

The history of the zone as a whole was affected by what was happening in Mesoamerica: the leadership, which in the Late Classic period lay with the northern sector, passed in the Post-Classic period to the southern sector.

Zone of South American Tradition

The archaeology of this zone contains so many gaps and obscurities that it seems unprofitable to seek to draw any conclusions at this stage. All that we can do is to note the recurrence in time and space of certain themes or objects which give the zone its unity—in spite of the diversity of local production and also, apparently, of features which can properly be described as regional. Thus in the field of sculpture we may note such common features as the theme of sacrifice by beheading, the tables decorated with a line of severed heads, the tables with openwork panels and the *metates* in the form of jaguars. In metal-working the same subjects—"eagles", frogs, monkeys, jaguars, human figures—are repeated throughout the whole extent of the zone.

In pottery we can distinguish two main traditions, whose origin is perhaps to be sought in northern Colombia and Venezuela, where they are found co-existing. The tradition of polychrome decoration is confined to southern Panama (Coclé, Azuero, Chiriquí) and southern Costa Rica. The tradition of incised and appliqué decoration is found throughout a much larger area, including the Antilles and half of Central America, from Veraguas to north-eastern Honduras.

CHRONOLOGICAL CHART

ZONE OF MESOAMERICAN TRADITION

Periods Maya area	Salvador	Ulúa-Yojoa	Comayagua	Choluteca	N.W. Costa Rica S.W. Nicaragua	Dates
						1500
Late Post-Classic		Naco		Malalaca	Late Polychrome	1400
						1300
						1200
Early Post-Classic	Cihuatán	Río Blanco	Las Vegas	Amapala	Middle Polychrome	1100
						1000
				Fonseca		900
			Lo de Vaca 3 and Yarumela 4			800
Late Classic	Tazumal and Los Llanitos	Yojoa			Early Polychrome	700
				San Lorenzo		600
						500
Early Classic	Tazumal Pre-Constructive			Chismuyo	Linear Decorated	400
						300
		Eden	Lo de Vaca 2 and Yarumela 3			200
						100 A
Late Pre-Classic					Zoned Bichrome	1 B
						100
						200
			Lo de Vaca 1 Yarumela 2			300
		Jaral				400
			Yarumela 1			500
Middle Pre-Classic						600
						700
						800
						900
						1000
Early Pre-Classic						1100
						1200
						1300
						1400
						1500
						1600
						1700
						1800
						1900
						2000
						2100
						2200

ZONE OF SOUTH AMERICAN TRADITION

Dates	N. Honduras	Central Costa Rica	Diquís-Chiriquí	Veraguas	Parita-Coclé
1500					
1400		Orosí	"Classic" Chiriquí	"Classic" Veraguas	Herrera
1300	Cocal				
1200		Chircot			
1100					Late Coclé
1000			San Lorenzo (Gulf)		
900					
800	Selin				
700					Early Coclé
600		Curridabat	Burica		Venado Beach 2
500					
400					Venado Beach 1? Santa María
300					
200					
D. 100			Scarified	Scarified Guacamayo	Scarified Guacamayo
1					
C. 100					
200					
300					
400					
500					
600					
700					
800					Sarigua
900					
1000					
1100					
1200					
1300					
1400					
1500					
1600					
1700					
1800					
1900					
2000					
2100					Monagrillo
2200					

NOTES

[1] For the purposes of this survey Central America, as an archaeological area showing a measure of unity, has as its northern boundary the southern limits of the Maya area during the Classic period. We thus exclude from consideration the Copán region and the upper Chamelecón valley in Honduras and the whole of Guatemala, which the Mayanists have always claimed as their own. On the other hand the territory of El Salvador comes within our field. Having regard to the existence of Pokomam enclaves (belonging to the Maya language family) in western Salvador at the time of the Conquest, some archaeologists put the Maya frontier on the Río Lempa, or perhaps farther west between the river and the Guatemalan border, though they still cannot accept Tazumal as a Classic Maya site. On the basis of the archaeological evidence and in the present state of knowledge, I find it difficult to regard western Salvador as being Maya; for the present, therefore, the whole of El Salvador is included in our survey. To the south the boundary of our area is drawn arbitrarily on the Colombian frontier. Since northwestern Colombia and eastern Panama are practically unexplored by archaeologists it is not possible at present to define any cultural frontier in these areas.

[2] We shall not follow the custom of including the Pacific zone in the Mesoamerican area and calling it the southern periphery of Mesoamerica. The large Mesoamerican cultural area is defined by a whole series of characteristics, including in particular such advanced traits as hieroglyphic writing, complex calendrical systems and stone architecture. Since the Pacific zone is "marginal" and has also many features in common with other parts of the isthmus, the drawing of a sharp line between Mesoamerica and non-Mesoamerica is unconvincing, even if we consider only the situation at the time of the Conquest. If we also consider the time factor we see in addition that the influence of the centres of civilisation tends to grow weaker with distance, and that the boundaries of the different cultural zones vary from one period to another. Thus it seems more appropriate, in discussing the Pacific zone, to talk only of a zone of Mesoamerican influence, defined as the zone in which influences of the Mesoamerican civilisations were manifested, to an extent which differed from one region to another and from one period to another.

[3] We have two carbon 14 datings. One, 90 ± 200 A.D., is associated with pottery of the Chombo phase, of the Chahuite Escondido sequence (Santa Elena peninsula). The other, 260 ± 70 A.D., dates the Catalina complex at the site of Ortega (Tempisque valley).

[4] The Zoned Bichrome types seem to have been influenced by pottery of the same period from south-western Costa Rica and Chiriquí, mainly decorated with hatched areas alternating with red painted areas (the Scarified type). Zelaya Trichrome can be compared only with pottery from the Central Valley and the Linea Vieja region in Costa Rica and with the Black-on-Buff variety of the Escotá Polychrome type in the Santa María complex (found at Girón, Parita, Panama). The origin of the first polychrome painting in black and white on red is to be sought in Panama, where we find similar polychrome types at Venado Beach, Sitio Conte, in the Azuero peninsula, and the province of Veraguas.

[5] In Costa Rica 565 ± 90; in Nicaragua (isthmus of Rivas), 572 ± 110, 582 ± 70 and, for the end of the period, 792 ± 120 A.D.

[6] The style of painting found on Carrillo and on some Galo vases (red motifs edged with black) has no equivalent in the north; in other respects it shows affinities with certain styles found in Panama (Venado Beach and Veraguas) which later gave birth to the style of the Alligator Ware of Chiriquí. Galo has also certain features in common with the pottery of Honduras —cylindrical vases with rectangular feet, vases with modelled monkeys' heads, figures of animals in silhouette on a black ground, jaguars in identical poses.

[7] See Stone 1957, fig. 54, A:b, b¹, fig. 45, A:a, and frontispiece.

[8] See John B. Glass, "Archaeological Survey of Western Honduras", in *Handbook of Middle American Indians*, Vol. 4, *Archaeological Frontiers and External Connections* (R. Wauchope, ed.), University of Texas Press, Austin, 1966.

[9] The end of the Early Polychrome period on the island of Ometepe (Nicaragua) is dated by carbon 14 to 792±120 A.D. Charcoal from Huerta del Aguacate (Guanacaste), associated with pottery of the Middle Polychrome period, has yielded a date of 970±70 A.D. Moreover the Mora Polychrome type shows a number of Late Classic features—painting in black and red on a light brown or orange ground, seated figures like those painted on Copador vases, the "Kan" cross, etc.

[10] Although the evidence is not yet sufficiently firm to allow us to date these statues with any certainty, we have a number of pointers which suggest a provisional dating in the Post-Classic period of Mesoamerican chronology. In a mound on the island of Zapatera, near which some statues were found, Squier excavated pottery which he describes as "fine material painted in brilliant colors". This brief annotation could readily be applied to the pottery of the Middle and Late Polychrome periods. On the same island, at Punta del Sapote, a collection of surface material by Norweb included numerous sherds of Papagayo Polychrome (Norweb, 1964). Finally certain pieces of sculpture at Papagayo (Bay of Culebra, Costa Rica), very similar to the statues on Lake Nicaragua, though smaller and more crudely executed, were still in position when the site was abandoned during the Late Polychrome period. Moreover on the evidence of the material in the museum at Juigalpa (Chontales), together with information supplied by Professor Gregorio Aguilar, director of the museum, the pottery from the sites where statues were found includes types dating from the Middle and Late Polychrome periods—Papagayo Polychrome, Jicote Polychrome, Mombacho Incised Polychrome, Palmares Incised, Vallejo Polychrome, etc. The museum also contains Zoned Bichrome pottery (particularly of the Bocana type) which is said to come from sites without statues. This evidence entitles us to include the east side of Lake Nicaragua in the zone of Mesoamerican tradition.

[11] E. G. Squier, *Nicaragua: its People, Scenery, Monuments and the Proposed Interoceanic Canal*, New York and London, 2 vols, 1852; Carl Bovallius, *Nicaraguan Antiquities*, Swedish Society of Anthropology and Geography, Stockholm, 1886.

[12] For the beginning of the period we have a carbon dating of 1120±70 A.D. from Chahuite Escondido.

[13] Matthew W. Stirling, "Exploring Ancient Panama by Helicopter", *National Geographic Magazine*, Vol. 97, No. 2, pp. 227–46 (illustrated), Washington, 1950.

[14] The Santa María complex at Girón includes trichrome ware with red and black painting on a light brown ground (Girón Polychrome and Escotá Polychrome). Rarely, two different colours are found on the same ground (e.g., the inside of a bowl may be painted red, while the outside, left in the natural buff, has a decoration of black lines), in a manner characteristic of the Zelaya Trichrome of Guanacaste. Some of the pottery recovered at Venado Beach (Canal Zone)—where we have two carbon 14 datings of 227 and 900 A.D.— is also, in my view, to be dated to Period IV: in particular the type which Lothrop calls Black-Line on Red and another type which may have given rise to the earliest polychrome ware in Guanacaste (López, decorated with black motifs edged by white lines on a red ground). The vases from the Diquís delta (Costa Rica), described by Lothrop under the name of the Parallel Line Incised type of Brown Ware,

can be assigned to Period IV on the basis of their form and decoration. In central and eastern Costa Rica the only material so far datable to Period IV consists of a number of pots with linear decoration in black on a red ground and some trichrome bowls showing affinities with Zelaya ware (Pl. 107). To these must be added the vases and figurines painted in purple on a light brown ground and incised which show close similarities with the Guinea Incised type of Guanacaste (Pl. 109).

[15] See Carl V. Hartman, "The Alligator as a Plastic Decorative Motive in Costa Rican Pottery", *American Anthropologist*, Vol. 9, No. 2, pp. 307–14 (illustrated), Lancaster, Pa, 1907; John H. Rowe, "Carl Hartman and his Place in the History of Archaeology", *Actas, 33⁰ Congreso Internacional de Americanistas*, San José, Vol. 2, pp. 268–79, 1959.

SELECT CRITICAL BIBLIOGRAPHY

GENERAL

Julian STEWARD (ed.), *Handbook of South American Indians*, Vol. 4, *The Circum-Caribbean Tribes*, Washington, 1948.

R. WAUCHOPE (ed.), *Handbook of Middle American Indians*, Vol. 4, *Archaeological Frontiers and External Connections*, University of Texas Press, Austin, 1966.

HONDURAS

1. North Coast and Bay Islands

William D. STRONG, *Archaeological Investigations in the Bay Islands, Spanish Honduras* (Smithsonian Miscellaneous Collections, Vol. 92, No. 14), 176 pp., Washington, 1935.
(A rapid reconnaissance of various sites on the Bay Islands, the north-eastern coast of Honduras and the Olancho valley. No stratigraphic excavations.)

Doris Z. STONE, *Archaeology of the North Coast of Honduras* (Memoirs of the Peabody Museum of Archaeology and Ethnology, Vol. 9, No. 1), 103 pp., Cambridge, Mass., 1941.
(A reconnaissance of the north coast, with excavations only at Travesia, in the Ulúa valley. Remains are systematically attributed to historically known tribes. No stratigraphy.)

Jeremiah F. EPSTEIN, *Late Ceramic Horizons in Northeastern Honduras* (Ph. D. dissertation, M.S.), University of Pennsylvania, 1957.
(Uses material and notes of unpublished excavations by Bird in 1937 and Ekholm and Kidder in 1950, and reconsiders Strong's work. Two ceramic complexes are distinguished.)

2. Central Honduras

William D. STRONG, Alfred KIDDER II and Paul DREXEL Jr, *Preliminary Report on the Smithsonian Institution—Harvard University Archaeological Expedition in Northwestern Honduras, 1936* (Smithsonian Miscellaneous Collections, Vol. 97, No. 1), Washington, 1938.
(A report—unfortunately only preliminary—on stratigraphic excavations on various sites in the Ulúa and Chamelecón valleys and the Lake Yojoa area. First outline of a ceramic sequence for north-western Honduras.)

Joel S. CANBY, *Excavations at Yarumela, Spanish Honduras* (Ph. D. dissertation, M.S.), Harvard University, 1949.

Joel S. CANBY, "Possible chronological implications of the long ceramic sequence recovered at Yarumela, Spanish Honduras", *The Civilizations of Ancient America: Selected Papers of the 29th International Congress of Americanists*, Vol. 1, pp. 79–85, Chicago, 1951.
(Preliminary report giving a resume of the ceramic sequence described in the unpublished thesis cited above.)

Doris Z. STONE, *The Archaeology of Central and Southern Honduras* (Papers of the Peabody Museum of Archaeology and Ethnology, Vol. 49, No. 3), 135 pp., Cambridge, Mass., 1957.
(A rapid reconnaissance of the various regions in central and southern Honduras. Few excavations, and always superficial. No stratigraphy.)

Claude F. BAUDEZ and Pierre BECQUELIN, "La séquence céramique de Los Naranjos, Honduras", *Akten des 38. Internationalen Amerikanisten-kongresses*, Stuttgart, 1968 (in the press).
(Gives the main results of a first season of field work.)

3. Southern Honduras

Claude F. BAUDEZ, "Niveaux céramiques au Honduras: une reconsidération de l'évolution culturelle", *Journal de la Société des Américanistes*, LV, 2, pp. 299–342, Paris, 1966.
(Preliminary results of stratigraphic excavations in the Gulf of Fonseca region and the Comayagua valley.)

EL SALVADOR

Samuel K. LOTHROP, "Pottery types and their sequence in El Salvador", *Indian Notes and Monographs* (Museum of the American Indian, Heye Foundation), Vol. 1, No. 4, pp. 165–220, New York, 1927.
(Evidence for two ceramic complexes at Cerro Zapote.)

John M. LONGYEAR III, *Archaeological Investigations in El Salvador* (Memoirs of the Peabody Museum of Archaeology and Ethnology, Vol. 9, No. 2), 90 pp., Cambridge, Mass., 1944.
(Includes a report on excavations at Los Llanitos, an inventory of sites in the country, and an appendix giving a brief report by S. Boggs on his excavations at Tazumal.)

Muriel N. PORTER DE MODEANO, "Material Preclásico de San Salvador", *Comunicaciones* (Instituto Tropical de Investigaciones Cientificas), IV, 3–4, pp. 105–112, San Salvador, 1955.
(Brief notes on the Pre-Classic material of Barranco Tovar.)

Wolfgang HABERLAND, "Ceramic sequences in El Salvador", *American Antiquity*, 26, 1, pp. 21–29, Salt Lake City, 1960.
(Very summary, and material not illustrated.)

NICARAGUA

Albert H. NORWEB, "Ceramic stratigraphy in southwestern Nicaragua", *Actas del 35. Congreso Internacional de Americanistas*, Vol. 1, pp. 551–561, Mexico City, 1962.
(Outline of the ceramic sequence of south-western Nicaragua.)

Wolfgang HABERLAND, (Notes or short articles, none longer than 5 pages, on the author's excavations on the island of Ometepe), 1959 to 1966.

COSTA RICA

Samuel K. LOTHROP, *Pottery of Costa Rica and Nicaragua* (Museum of the American Indian, Heye Foundation, Contributions, Vol. 8), 2 vol., 487 pp., New York, 1962.
(Descriptions and illustrations of decorated pottery from collections obtained from sources other than scientifically conducted excavations.)

1. North-Western Costa Rica

Carl V. HARTMAN, *Archaeological Researches on the Pacific Coast of Costa Rica* (Pittsburgh Carnegie Museum Memoirs, Vol. 3, No. 1), 188 pp., Pittsburgh, 1907.
(Excavation of the famous cemetery of Las Huacas, and publication of material in private collections.)

Michael D. COE, "Preliminary report on archaeological investigations in coastal Guanacaste, Costa Rica", *Akten des 34. Internationalen Amerikanistenkongresses*, pp. 358–365, Vienna, 1962.
(Outline of the ceramic sequence of the Pacific coast of Guanacaste.)

Claude F. BAUDEZ, *Recherches archéologiques dans la vallée du Tempisque, Guanacaste, Costa Rica* (Travaux et Mémoires de l'Institut des Hautes Etudes de l'Amérique latine, No. 18), 401 pp., Paris, 1967.
(Ceramic sequence of the region.)

2. *Central Costa Rica*

Carl V. HARTMAN, *Archaeological Researches in Costa Rica* (Publications of the Royal Ethnographical Museum, Stockholm), 195 pp., Stockholm, 1901.
(Excavations of cemeteries in the Cartago valley and Linea Vieja region.)

3. *Southern Costa Rica*

Wolfgang HABERLAND, *Archäologische Untersuchungen in Südost Costa Rica* (Acta Humboldtiana, Series Geographica and Ethnographica, No. 1), 81 pp., Wiesbaden, 1959.
(Two ceramic complexes are distinguished.)

Samuel K. LOTHROP, *Archaeology of the Diquís Delta* (Papers of the Peabody Museum of Archaeology and Ethnology, Vol. 51), 142 pp., Cambridge, Mass., **1963.**
(Stratigraphy of limited value; very poor deposits and defective typology.)

PANAMA

1. *Chiriquí*

Olga LINARES DE SAPIR, *Cultural Chronology of the Gulf of Chiriquí, Panama* (Smithsonian Contributions to Anthropology, Vol. 8), 119 pp., Smithsonian Institution, Washington, 1968.
(A thorough study of a region whose cultural poverty suggests that it was marginal to developments in the Chiriquí highlands.)

2. *Veraguas*

Samuel K. LOTHROP, *The Archaeology of Southern Veraguas, Panama* (Memoirs of the Peabody Museum of Archaeology and Ethnology, Vol. 9, No. 3), 116 pp., Cambridge, Mass., 1950.
(Publication of material from excavation of tombs.)

3. Coclé and Parita

Samuel K. LOTHROP, *Coclé: an Archaeological Study of Central Panama* (Memoirs of the Peabody Museum of Archaeology and Ethnology, Vols. 7 and 8), 2 vol., 327 and 292 pp., Cambridge, Mass., 1937–1942.
(Mainly devoted to the rich cemetery of Sitio Conte.)

Gordon R. WILLEY and Charles R. McGIMSEY III, *The Monagrillo Culture of Panama* (Papers of the Peabody Museum of Archaeology and Ethnology, Vol. 49, No. 2), 158 pp., Cambridge, Mass., 1954.
(An excellent monograph on the oldest ceramic complex so far discovered in Central America. Other complexes of later date are also described and their stratigraphic position determined.)

Gordon R. WILLEY and T. STODDARD, "Cultural stratigraphy in Panama: a preliminary report on the Girón site", *American Antiquity*, 19, 4, pp. 332–343, Menasha, 1954.
(Completes the Parita regional sequence.)

Charles R. McGIMSEY III, "Cerro Mangote: a preceramic site in Panama", *American Antiquity*, 22, 2, Pt 1, pp. 151–161, Menasha, 1956.
(Report on the oldest—pre-ceramic—site so far excavated in Central America.)

John LADD, *Archaeological Investigations in the Parita and Santa Maria Zones of Panama* (Bureau of American Ethnology, Bulletin No. 193), 291 pp., Smithsonian Institution, Washington, 1964.
(Pottery typology and sequence, based on material excavated by Stirling and Willey twenty years before.)

4. Darien

Sigwald LINNÉ, *Darien in the Past: the Archaeology of Eastern Panama and Northwestern Colombia*, Göteborg, 1929.
(Very rapid reconnaissance without stratigraphic excavation; little usable information.)

LIST OF ILLUSTRATIONS

1 Olmec rock carving. Height about 180 cm. From Hacienda Las Victorias, near Chalchuapa, western Salvador. Period I (before 200 B.C.). Still in situ.

2 Pottery bowl with Usulután decoration in orange and cream. Diameter 26 cm. From Santa María, Usulután, eastern Salvador. Period II (200 B.C. to 550 A.D.). Museo Nacional, San Salvador, Salvador.

3 Pottery bowl with four mammiform feet; Usulután decoration. Height 15 cm. Provenance unknown. Period II (0-550 A.D.). Museo Nacional, San Salvador, El Salvador.

4 Anthropomorphic jar with Usulután decoration, peccary's head at base of spout. Height 26 cm. From León region, Nicaragua. Period II (200 B.C. to 550 A.D.). Collection of Enrique Neret, Managua, Nicaragua.

5 Tripod bowl with Usulután decoration; the head, feet and tail of an animal are represented round the rim. Length 17 cm. From Managua area, Nicaragua. Period II (200 B.C. to 550 A.D.). Collection of Enrique Neret, Managua, Nicaragua.

6 Tetrapod bowl with incised and Usulután decoration representing a frog. Height 9.5 cm. From Comayagua valley, Honduras. Period II (200 B.C. to 550 A.D.). Collection of Banco Atlántida, Tegucigalpa, Honduras.

7 Effigy vase. Height 20 cm. From Chinandega, northern Nicaragua. Period II (200 B.C. to 550 A.D.). Collection of Enrique Neret, Managua, Nicaragua.

8 Buff pottery figurine (solid). Height 11 cm. From eastern Salvador. Period II (200 B.C. to 550 A.D.). Collection of Walter Soundy, Santa Tecla, El Salvador.

9 Pottery figurine (solid), painted light orange. Height 29 cm. From Laguna de Chalchuapa, western Salvador. Period II (200 B.C. to 550 A.D.). Collection of Tomás de Vilanova, Santa Tecla, El Salvador.

10 Mother and child: red pottery figurine (solid), with traces of white paint. Height 17 cm. From San Agustín, eastern Salvador. Period II (200 B.C. to 550 A.D.). Collection of Walter Soundy, Santa Tecla, El Salvador.

11   Hollow pottery figurine with white painting and Usulután decoration. Height 16.5 cm. From Chichigalpa, northern Nicaragua. Period II (200 B.C. to 550 A.D.). Collection of Enrique Neret, Managua, Nicaragua.

12   Pottery jar, buff, with relief figure of a monkey between panels of red painted and incised ornament; red lines on neck. Height 16.5 cm. From El Hacha, Guanacaste, Costa Rica. Period II (300 B.C. to 300 A.D.). Private collection, San José, Costa Rica.

13   Bottle-shaped jar of buff pottery, with areas painted in red within incised lines. Height 22 cm. From Granada area, Nicaragua. Period II (300 B.C. to 300 A.D.). Collection of Enrique Neret, Managua, Nicaragua.

14   Spherical ocarina, four-holed, with an animal's head (jaguar and coati) at each end; blackish-brown ware with bands of punctated decoration. Length 14 cm. From Guanacaste province, Costa Rica. Period II (300 B.C. to 300 A.D.). Private collection, San José, Costa Rica.

15   Pottery jar with Zoned Bichrome decoration. Height 23 cm. From Guanacaste province, Costa Rica. Period II (300 B.C. to 300 A.D.). Collection of Juan Dada, San José, Costa Rica.

16   Pottery jar decorated with the outline of a headless figure painted in black on a red ground within a double incised line. Height 32 cm. From León area, Nicaragua. Period II (300 B.C. to 300 A.D.). Collection of Enrique Neret, Managua, Nicaragua.

17   Pot-stand, open at both ends: light brown ware with incised and red painted ornament. Height 28 cm. From León area, Nicaragua. Period II (300 B.C. to 300 A.D.). Collection of Enrique Neret, Managua, Nicaragua.

18   Hollow pottery figurine. Height 24 cm. From Nicoya area, Guanacaste, Costa Rica. Period II (300 B.C. to 300 A.D.). Museo Nacional, San José, Costa Rica.

19   Statuette (hollow) of red ware. Height 34 cm. From La Guinea, Guanacaste, Costa Rica. Period II (0-500 A.D.). Collection of Evelyn de Goicoechea, San José, Costa Rica.

20   *Bowl of orange-red ware: woman and child in a hammock hanging from a snake. Diameter 19 cm. From Filadelfia, Guanacaste, Costa Rica. Period II (0-500 A.D.). Private collection, San José, Costa Rica.*

21   *Tripod bowl representing the "royal" vulture* (Zopilote Rey): *orange-red surface with incised geometric decoration. Height (to head) 13 cm. From Guanacaste province, Costa Rica. Period II (0-500 A.D.). Collection of Evelyn de Goicoechea, San José, Costa Rica.*

22   *Pottery jar. Height 29.5 cm. From El Viejo, Guanacaste, Costa Rica. Period II (300-500 A.D.). Collection of Evelyn de Goicoechea, San José, Costa Rica.*

23   *Pottery jar, with handles of jar and lid in the form of jaguars. From Guanacaste province, Costa Rica. Period II (300-500 A.D.). Collection of Marjorie de Oduber, San José, Costa Rica.*

24   *Basalt* metate *with bird's head. Length 72 cm. From Nosará, Guanacaste, Costa Rica. Period unknown. Private collection, San José, Costa Rica.*

25   *Basalt* metate *with bird's head turned to one side. Length 41 cm. From Guanacaste province, Costa Rica. Period unknown. Private collection, San José, Costa Rica.*

26   *Jadeite pendants from Costa Rica: human figures, an owl and a bat. The largest is 16.5 cm. high. Above, from Linea Vieja;* below, right, *from Río Cuarto de Alajuela; the others, from Guanacaste province. Period unknown. Private collection, San José, Costa Rica.*

27   *Mace-heads of chalcedony in the form of birds. Length 14 and 15 cm. From Lagarto, Guanacaste, Costa Rica. Private collection, San José, Costa Rica.*

28   *Pottery jar: monkey holding a fruit. Greatest height 21 cm. From Tazumal, El Salvador. End of Period II (300-550 A.D.). Museo Nacional, San Salvador, El Salvador.*

29   *Ruins of Tazumal, near Chalchuapa, El Salvador: northern front of Structure I. Periods III and IV.*

30   *Copador bowl: reclining figure under a frieze of "false glyphs". Diameter 17 cm. From Tazumal, El Salvador. Period III (550-950 A.D.). Museo Nacional, San Salvador, El Salvador.*

31 *Copador bowl. Diameter 20 cm. From Costa del Balsamo, La Libertad, El Salvador. Period III (550-950 A.D.). Collection of Walter Soundy, Santa Tecla, El Salvador.*

32 *Pottery jar: figure seated between two conventional representations of a ball court. Height 19 cm. From eastern Salvador. Period III (550-950 A.D.). Collection of Walter Soundy, Santa Tecla, El Salvador.*

33 *Pottery jar decorated with interlinked figures. Height 20 cm. From Aguacate, Lake Yojoa, Honduras. Period III (550-950 A.D.). Private collection.*

34 *Pottery jar; the main decorative theme is the head of a mythological animal, with a frieze of birds round the rim. Height 17 cm. From Tazumal, El Salvador. Period III (550-950 A.D.). Museo Nacional, San Salvador, El Salvador.*

35-38 *Pottery jar: continuous pattern of decoration, showing meetings between dignitaries. Height 24 cm. From Tenampua, Comayagua valley, Honduras. Period III (550-950 A.D.). Collection of René Sempé, Tegucigalpa, Honduras.*

39 *Pottery jar: dancing monkey. Height 21 cm. From Nejapá, Department of San Salvador, El Salvador. Period III (550-950 A.D.). Collection of Tomás de Vilanova, Santa Tecla, El Salvador.*

40 *Pottery bowl decorated in Usulután technique and polychrome painting, depicting a monkey. Diameter 16 cm. From Tazumal, El Salvador. Period III (550-950 A.D.). Museo Nacional, San Salvador, El Salvador.*

41 *Pottery jar: scene of homage (?). Height 23 cm. From Tenampua, Comayagua valley, Honduras. Period III (550-950 A.D.). Collection of Mary de Agurcia, Tegucigalpa, Honduras.*

42 *Polychrome jar, depicting an owl. Height 13 cm. From Honduras. Period III (550-950 A.D.). Collection of Banco Atlántida, Tegucigalpa, Honduras.*

43 *Polychrome vase depicting a bird. Height 23 cm. From Department of San Miguel, eastern Salvador. Period III (550-950 A.D.). Collection of Walter Soundy, Santa Tecla, El Salvador.*

44 *Pottery vase with polychrome decoration and monkey's head modelled in relief. Height 14 cm. From San Jacinto, Department of San Salvador, El Salvador. Period III (550-950 A.D.). Collection of Walter Soundy, Santa Tecla, El Salavdor.*

45 *Pottery jar, with the conventional sign for the jaws of Tlaloc painted in black on a light brown ground and with areas of white-painted spikes. Height 17 cm. From Tenampua, Comayagua valley, Honduras. Period III (550-950 A.D.). Private collection, Tegucigalpa, Honduras.*

46 *Jar of light brown ware, with a monkey's head on the neck. Height 25 cm. Provenance unknown. Period III (550-950 A.D.). Museo Nacional, San Salvador, El Salvador.*

47 *Pottery vase with polychrome decoration: conventional representations, including Maya features (woven mat, "Kan" cross). Height 19 cm. From Ahuachapan area, western Salvador. Period III (550-950 A.D.). Collection of Dolly de Mena Ariz, Santa Tecla, El Salvador.*

48 *Pottery jar in the form of a human head, painted in purple and orange on a light brown ground. Height 18 cm. Provenance unknown. Period III (550-950 A.D.). Collection of Banco Atlántida, Tegucigalpa, Honduras.*

49 *Bowl of light brown ware with carved decoration. Diameter 13 cm. From Department of San Salvador, El Salvador. Period III (550-950 A.D.). Museo Nacional, San Salvador, El Salvador.*

50 *Basalt* hacha, *showing a human head upside down in a jaguar's jaws. Dimensions 23 × 22 cm. Provenance unknown. Period III (550-950 A.D.). Museo Nacional ,San Salvador, El Salvador.*

51 *Basalt* palma. *Height 53 cm. From Laguna de Chalchuapa, El Salvador. Period III (550-950 A.D.). Collection of Tomás de Vilanova, Santa Tecla, El Salvador.*

52 *Pottery vase: two-headed crocodile. Height 16 cm. From Nacascolo, Guanacaste, Costa Rica. Period III (500-800 A.D.). Collection of Juan Dada, San José, Costa Rica.*

53 *Pottery jar with annular base. Height 24 cm. From Arenal de Tilarán, Guanacaste, Costa Rica. Period III (500-800 A.D.). Private collection, San José, Costa Rica.*

54 Pottery jar with jaguar heads modelled in relief and two-headed crocodile as principal decorative theme. Height 21 cm. From Nacascolo, Guanacaste, Costa Rica. Period III (500-800 A.D.). Collection of Juan Dada, San José, Costa Rica.

55 Hollow pottery statuette. Height 24 cm. From Nacascolo, Guanacaste, Costa Rica. Period III (500-800 A.D.). Collection of Juan Dada, San José, Costa Rica.

56 Basalt stela: figure with headdress in the form of Tlaloc's head, holding a sceptre or ceremonial bar. Height 270 cm. From Tazumal, El Salvador. Probably Period IV (950-1200 A.D.). Museo Nacional, San Salvador, El Salvador.

57 Hollow pottery statuette, with remains of painting in black, red and orange on a cream ground. Height 38 cm. From Department of Usulután, El Salvador. Period IV (950-1200 A.D.). Collection of Tomás de Vilanova, Santa Tecla, El Salvador.

58 Jar in the form of a deer; Tohil Plumbate ware. Height 17 cm. From eastern Salvador. Period IV (950-1200 A.D.). Collection of Walter Soundy, Santa Tecla, El Salvador.

59 Pottery vase: figure with spear-thrower. Height 24 cm. From Chalchuapa, El Salvador. Period IV (950-1200 A.D.). Collection of Tomás de Vilanova, Santa Tecla, El Salvador.

60 Bowl of buff ware, with incised motifs on a band of purple painting. Height 13 cm. From Department of La Paz, El Salvador. Period IV (950-1200 A.D.). Museo Nacional, San Salvador. El Salvador.

61 Tripod bowl of buff ware with red painting. Diameter 25 cm. Provenance unknown. Period IV (950-1200 A.D.). Museo Nacional, San Salvador, El Salvador.

62 Jar with head of Tlaloc; Tohil Plumbate ware. Height 16.5 cm. From Chalchuapa area, El Salvador. Period IV (950-1200 A.D.). Collection of Tomás de Vilanova, Santa Tecla, El Salvador.

63 Jug of red ware with head of Tlaloc. Height 20 cm. Provenance unknown. Period IV (950-1200 A.D.). Museo Nacional, San Salvador, El Salvador.

64   *Zoomorphic jar (jaguar?). Height 30 cm. From Filadelfia, Guanacaste, Costa Rica. Period IV (800-1200 A.D.) (?). Museo Nacional, San José, Costa Rica.*

65   *Tripod bowl, polychrome: the upper jaw of a feathered serpent. Diameter 24 cm. From southern Nicaragua. Period IV (800-1200 A.D.). Collection of Mario Belli, Managua, Nicaragua.*

66   *Pottery bowl with black and orange painting on a cream ground: a mask? Height 12 cm. From southern Nicaragua. Period IV (800-1200 A.D.). Collection of Mario Belli, Managua, Nicaragua.*

67   *Pottery vase: man with a spear-thrower. Height 21 cm. From Panamá, Guanacaste, Costa Rica. Period IV (800-1200 A.D.). Collection of Marjorie de Oduber, San José, Costa Rica.*

68   *Pottery vase: man on his knees carrying a load with the help of a* mecapal *(leather band round the forehead). Height 24 cm. From southern Nicaragua. Period IV (800-1200 A.D.). Collection of Mario Belli, Managua, Nicaragua.*

69   *Inside of tripod bowl: geometric motifs and jaguars painted in red, grey and black on a cream ground. Diameter 26 cm. From southern Nicaragua. Period IV (800-1200 A.D.). Collection of Mario Belli, Managua, Nicaragua.*

70   *Inside of tripod bowl: black and orange painting on a cream ground (jaguars' and serpents' heads). Diameter 22 cm. From southern Nicaragua. Period IV (800-1200 A.D.). Collection of Mario Belli, Managua, Nicaragua.*

71   *Pottery jar: a mask? Height 30 cm. From Nacascolo, Guanacaste, Costa Rica. Period IV (800-1200 A.D.). Collection of Juan Dada, San José, Costa Rica.*

72   *Pottery jar. Height 14.5 cm. From La Guinea, Guanacaste, Costa Rica. Period IV or V. Private collection, San José, Costa Rica.*

73   *Incense-burner with cover: the bowl is borne on the back of a jaguar, and there is another on the cover. Light brown ware with white painting on rows of spikes. Height 51 cm. From province of Guanacaste, Costa Rica. Period IV (800-1200 A.D.). Private collection, San José, Costa Rica.*

74 Incense-burner with cover: two-headed crocodile on the cover. Light brown ware, with appliqué and white painted decoration. Height 42 cm. From Guanacaste province, Costa Rica. Period IV (800-1200 A.D.). Private collection, San José, Costa Rica.

75 Hollow pottery figurine. Height 18 cm. From Nacascolo, Guanacaste, Costa Rica. Period IV (800-1200 A.D.). Private collection, San José, Costa Rica.

76 Hollow pottery statuette of a jaguar: black and orange painting on a white ground. Height 19 cm. From southern Nicaragua. Period IV (800-1200 A.D.). Collection of Mario Belli, Managua, Nicaragua.

77 Hollow pottery statuette of a female crocodile (?), seated: black, orange and red painting on a cream ground. Height 20 cm. From Mombacho, near Granada, Nicaragua. Period IV (800-1200 A.D.). Collection of Enrique Neret, Managua, Nicaragua.

78 Basalt statue: man and crocodile. Height 190 cm. From the island of Pensacola, Lake Nicaragua. Period IV (800-1200 A.D.) (?). Colegio Centro-América, Granada, Nicaragua.

79 Basalt statue: a man standing with a small jaguar on his shoulders. Total height 175 cm.; visible height 145 cm. From Punta del Sapote, island of Zapatera, Lake Nicaragua. Period IV (800-1200 A.D.) (?). Colegio Centro-América, Granada, Nicaragua.

80 Basalt statue: figure seated on a slit drum. Present height 180 cm. From Punta de las Figuras, island of Zapatera, Lake Nicaragua. Period IV (800-1200 A.D.) (?). Colegio Centro-América, Granada, Nicaragua.

81 Basalt statue on column: man wearing a helmet in the form of a bird's head. Height 225 cm. From Punta del Sapote, island of Zapatera, Lake Nicaragua. Period IV (800-1200 A.D.) (?). Colegio Centro-América, Granada, Nicaragua.

82 Basalt statue: man with shield, wearing an animal mask. Height 175 cm. Provenance unknown. Period IV (800-1200 A.D.) (?). Colegio Centro-América, Granada, Nicaragua.

83 *Basalt statue: man with a crocodile's head on his shoulders. Height 150 cm. From Punta del Sapote, island of Zapatera, Lake Nicaragua. Period IV (800-1200 A.D.) (?). Colegio Centro-América, Granada, Nicaragua.*

84 *Basalt statue: standing figure wearing a loincloth, with a snake's head below the belt. Present height 160 cm. From Santa Matilde, Department of Chontales, Nicaragua. Period IV (800-1200 A.D.) (?). Juigalpa Museum, Chontales, Nicaragua.*

85 *Basalt statue. Height 250 cm. From Copelito, Department of Chontales, Nicaragua. Period IV (800-1200 A.D.) (?). Juigalpa Museum, Chontales, Nicaragua.*

86 *Basalt statue. Height 200 cm. From El Salto, Department of Chontales, Nicaragua. Period IV (800-1200 A.D.) (?). Juigalpa Museum, Chontales, Nicaragua.*

87 *Basalt statue. Present height 172 cm. From Hacienda El Carmen, Department of Chontales, Nicaragua. Period IV (800-1200 A.D.) (?). Juigalpa Museum, Chontales, Nicaragua.*

88 *Basalt statue. Present height 480 cm. From San Pedro de Lóvago, Department of Chontales, Nicaragua. Period IV (800-1200 A.D.) (?). Juigalpa Museum, Chontales, Nicaragua.*

89 *Basalt statue. Present height 222 cm. From San Pedro de Lóvago, Department of Chontales, Nicaragua. Period IV (800-1200 A.D.) (?). Juigalpa Museum, Chontales, Nicaragua.*

90 *Gold pendant: crocodile. Length 8 cm. From Puntarenas area, Guanacaste, Costa Rica. Period IV or V. Private collection, San José, Costa Rica.*

91 *Tripod bowl with red painting on a buff ground. Diameter 18 cm. From Olancho valley, Honduras. Period V (1200-1525 A.D.). Collection of Banco Atlántida, Tegucigalpa, Honduras.*

92 *Pottery vase. Height 24 cm. From Nacascolo, Guanacaste, Costa Rica. Period V (1200-1525 A.D.). Collection of Juan Dada, San José, Costa Rica.*

93　Pottery bowl: feathered serpent. Height 15 cm. From Guanacaste province, Costa Rica. Period V (1200-1525 A.D.). Private collection, San José, Costa Rica.

94　Jar with small jaguar on neck: blackish-brown ware with incised decoration. Height 30 cm. From Nacascolo, Guanacaste, Costa Rica. Period V (1200-1525 A.D.). Private collection, San José, Costa Rica.

95　Jar in the form of a bird: blackish-brown ware with incised decoration. Length 20 cm. From Nacascolo, Guanacaste, Costa Rica. Period V (1200-1525 A.D.). Collection of Juan Dada, San José, Costa Rica.

96-97　Pottery vase with painted and incised decoration: crocodile (?) and Earth Monster. Height 20 cm. From Nacascolo, Guanacaste, Costa Rica. Period V (1200-1525 A.D.). Private collection, San José, Costa Rica.

98　Pottery vase. Height 34 cm. From Caña de Castilla, southern Nicaragua. Period V (1200-1525 A.D.). Collection of Enrique Neret, Managua, Nicaragua.

99　Wooden axe handle: vulture perched on a branch. Length 36 cm. From Punta de Chiltepe, Lake Nicaragua. Period unknown. Museo Nacional, Managua, Nicaragua.

100　Vase of brown ware with depressed base and incised decoration: lizard climbing. Height 23.5 cm. From Concepción, Chiriquí, Panama. Period III (300 B.C. to 300 A.D.). Collection of Guillermo Trujillo, Panamá, Panamá.

101　Tripod bowl with melon grooves between areas of coarse hatching: light red ware, with rim painted in dark red. Height 12 cm. From Concepción, Chiriquí, Panamá. Period III (300 B.C. to 300 A.D.). Collection of Guillermo Trujillo, Panamá, Panamá.

102　Vase of brown Guacamayo type: red painting on rim and lower part of vase. Height 30 cm. From Tonosí, Los Santos province, Panamá. Period III (300 B.C. to 300 A.D.). Canavaggio collection, Panamá, Panamá.

103　Vase of brown ware with incised decoration: a "humanised" hammerhead shark, head downwards. Height 30 cm. From Barriles, Chiriquí, Panamá. Period III (300 B.C. to 300 A.D.). Collection of Guillermo Trujillo, Panamá, Panamá.

104   *Basalt statue: "victor" and "vanquished". Total height 220 cm. From Barriles, Chiriquí, Panamá. Period III (300 B.C. to 300 A.D.). Museo Nacional, Panamá, Panamá.*

105   *Basalt statue: "sacrificer". Present height 160 cm. From Barriles, Chiriquí, Panamá. Period III (300 B.C. to 300 A.D.). Museo Nacional, Panamá, Panamá.*

106   *Basalt table with a line of human heads round the edge. Length 217 cm. From Barriles, Chiriquí, Panamá. Period III (300 B.C. to 300 A.D.). Museo Nacional, Panamá, Panamá.*

107   *Bowl of buff ware: black lines on upper part, rim and lower part painted in red. Diameter 21 cm. From Guápiles, Linea Vieja, Costa Rica. Period IV (300-500 A.D.). Museo Nacional, San José, Costa Rica.*

108   *Vase of buff ware: highly stylised birds painted in red and edged with an incised line. Height 43 cm. From Barriles, Chiriquí, Panamá. Period III (300 B.C. to 300 A.D.). Museo Nacional, Panamá, Panamá.*

109   *Bird-headed jar: incised decoration and purple painting on a brown ground. Height 18 cm. From Guácimo, Linea Vieja, Costa Rica. Periods III-IV (0-500 A.D.). Private collection, San José, Costa Rica.*

110   *Hollow pottery statuette: figure presenting or reading a tablet (painting worn off). Height 22 cm. From Carbonera, southern Costa Rica. Probably Period III or IV (0-500 A.D.). Private collection, San José, Costa Rica.*

111   *Jar in shape of a turtle: red painting and black patterns on a white ground. Height 14 cm. From Río Grande, Coclé, Panamá. Early Coclé style. Period V (500-800 A.D.). Museo Nacional, Panamá, Panamá.*

112-113   *Hollow pottery statuette: man drinking, reclining in a chair similar to the duhos of the Antilles. Length 26 cm. From Santiago, Veraguas, Panamá. Early Coclé style. Period V (500-800 A.D.). Díaz collection, Panamá, Panamá.*

114   *Vase of buff ware: appliqué decoration and relief figures of animals, lower part painted red. Height 13 cm. From Guácimo, Linea Vieja, Costa Rica. Period V (500-800 A.D.). Museo Nacional, San José, Costa Rica.*

115 *Jar of brown ware: vultures devouring bodies. Height 22 cm. From Linea Vieja, Costa Rica. Period V (500-800 A.D.). Museo Nacional, San José, Costa Rica.*

116 *Pottery jar: crocodile's head, upside down. Height 26 cm. From Río de Jesús, Veraguas, Panamá. Period VI (800-1525 A.D.). Collection of Guillermo Trujillo, Panamá, Panamá.*

117 *Zoomorphic jar. Height 22 cm. From Parita area, Panamá. Period VI (800-1525 A.D.). Museo Nacional, Panamá, Panamá.*

118 *Inside of pottery dish with annular base: crocodiles facing one another. Diameter 26 cm. From Parita, Panamá. Period VI (800-1525 A.D.). Museo Nacional, Panamá, Panamá.*

119 *Inside of a pedestal dish: a crocodile standing erect, painted in several colours. Diameter 28 cm. From Soná, Veraguas, Panamá. Period VI (800-1525 A.D.). Ferrari collection, Panamá, Panamá.*

120 *Inside of a pedestal plate: hammerhead shark. Diameter 24 cm. From Parita area, Panamá. Period VI (800-1525 A.D.). Ferrari collection, Panamá, Panamá.*

121 *Pendants of agate and marine ivory. The largest is 18 cm. long. From Soná, Veraguas, except the dog, which is from La Mura, near Parita, Panamá. Period VI (800-1525 A.D.). Ferrari collection, Panamá, Panamá.*

122 *Pectoral plaque of gold foil, repoussé: jaguars confronting one another. Diameter 11 cm. From Veraguas province, Panamá. Period VI (800-1525 A.D.). Museo Nacional, Panamá, Panamá.*

123 *Pendant of* tumbaga: *two-headed figure brandishing a two-headed serpent. Height 8 cm. From Veraguas province, Panamá. Period VI (800-1525 A.D.). Museo Nacional, Panamá, Panamá.*

124 *Hollow pottery figurine: mother and child. Height 13 cm. From Congo, Osa peninsula, southern Costa Rica. Period VI (800-1525 A.D.). Museo Nacional, San José, Costa Rica.*

125 *Pottery vase with negative painting. Height 16 cm. From Bugaba, Chiriquí, Panamá. Period VI (800-1525 A.D.). Collection of Guillermo Trujillo, Panamá, Panamá.*

126 *Pottery vase: jaguar heads on handles, with a crocodile as the main decorative theme. Height 21 cm. From Hatillo, southern Costa Rica. Period VI (800-1525 A.D.). Museo Nacional, San José, Costa Rica.*

127 *Jar in the form of a bird (an owl?), with removable head. Height 20 cm. From southern Costa Rica. Period VI (800-1525 A.D.). Collection of Marjorie de Oduber, San José, Costa Rica.*

128 *Pottery ocarina in the form of a crocodile. Length 21 cm. From southern Costa Rica. Period VI (800-1525 A.D.). Collection of Marjorie de Oduber, San José, Costa Rica.*

129 *Pottery ear ornaments, representing a jaguar and a bird. Length 12 and 13 cm. From Aguas Zarcas, San Carlos plain, Costa Rica. Period VI (800-1525 A.D.). Collection of Evelyn de Goicoechea, San José, Costa Rica.*

130 *Gold pendants. The largest is 6 cm. long. From the Diquís delta, Costa Rica. Period VI (800-1525 A.D.) (?). Private collection, San José, Costa Rica.*

131 *Gold pendant. Length 6 cm. From Palmar, southern Costa Rica. Period VI (800-1525 A.D.) (?). Private collection, San José, Costa Rica.*

132 *Two gold pendants; one of them represents a victim. Height 7 cm. From southern Costa Rica. Period VI (800-1525 A.D.) (?). Private collection, San José, Costa Rica.*

133 *Round stool of buff pottery: hybrid of man, bird and jaguar. Height 11 cm. From Boquete, Chiriquí, Panamá. Period VI (800-1525 A.D.). Museo Nacional, Panamá, Panamá.*

134 *Vase of buff ware with feet in the form of fishes. Height 18 cm. From Chiriquí province, Panamá. Period VI (800-1525 A.D.). Museo Nacional, Panamá, Panamá.*

135 *Vase of light brown ware, with small figures of dogs on each of the feet. Height 29 cm. From Chiriquí province, Panamá. Period V or VI. Museo Nacional, Panamá, Panamá.*

136 *Vase of buff ware with pointed base; two figures of monkeys modelled in relief. Height 20 cm. From Concepción, Chiriquí, Panamá. Period VI (800-1525 A.D.). Museo Nacional, Panamá, Panamá.*

137   Bowl of light brown ware, with feet in the form of three female figures, each suffering from a different complaint (one in the head, another in the abdomen, the third in the breast). Height 18 cm. From Chiriquí province, Panamá. Period VI (800-1525 A.D.). Collection of Guillermo Trujillo, Panamá, Panamá.

138   Statue in soft sandstone: jaguar. Length 28 cm. From Puerto Cortés, southern Costa Rica. Period VI (800-1525 A.D.). Museo Nacional, San José, Costa Rica.

139   Statue in soft sandstone. Height 22 cm. From the Diquís delta, Costa Rica. Period VI (800-1525 A.D.). Private collection, San José, Costa Rica.

140   Statue in soft sandstone: figure with jaguar's head. Height 38 cm. From the Diquís delta, Costa Rica. Period VI (800-1525 A.D.). Private collection, San José, Costa Rica.

141   Statue in soft sandstone. Height 24 cm. From the Diquís delta, Costa Rica. Period VI (800-1525 A.D.). Private collection, San José, Costa Rica.

142   Tripod bowl of brown ware with hollow feet, representing a man emerging, head downwards, from the jaws of a monster. Diameter 35 cm. From Paso del Tigre, Siquírres, Linea Vieja, Costa Rica. Period VI (800-1525 A.D.). Collection of Evelyn de Goicoechea, San José, Costa Rica.

143   Tripod bowl of light brown ware with feet in the form of owls. Height 24 cm. From Guácimo, Linea Vieja, Costa Rica. Period VI (800-1525 A.D.). Private collection, San José, Costa Rica.

144   Basalt statuettes: two figures of children with axes and severed heads. Height 21 and 23 cm. From Guácimo, Linea Vieja, Costa Rica. Period VI (800-1525 A.D.). Private collection, San José, Costa Rica.

145   Hollow figurine of red pottery. Height 30 cm. From Aguas Zarcas, San Carlos plain, Costa Rica. Period VI (800-1525 A.D.). Collection of Evelyn de Goicoechea, San José, Costa Rica.

146-147   Basalt statuette: man with a severed head dangling from a rope. Height 25 cm. From Río Verde, Limón province, Costa Rica. Period VI (800-1525 A.D.). Private collection, San José, Costa Rica.

148   Basalt statuette: a prisoner. Height 50 cm. From Linea Vieja, Costa Rica. Period VI (800-1525 A.D.). Private collection, San José, Costa Rica.

149 *Basalt statuette: man wearing a crocodile mask. Height 30 cm. From Linea Vieja, Costa Rica. Period VI (800-1525 A.D.). Private collection, San José, Costa Rica.*

150 *Basalt statuette: seated figure of a man smoking. Height 26 cm. From Pocosí area, Limón province, Costa Rica. Period VI (800-1525 A.D.). Museo Nacional, San José, Costa Rica.*

151 *Basalt table, with openwork panel and white painting. Length 74 cm. From Guápiles, Linea Vieja, Costa Rica. Period VI (800-1525 A.D.). Private collection, San José, Costa Rica.*

152 *Basalt* metate *in the form of a jaguar; Atlas figures of small jaguars between the legs. Length 36 cm. From Las Mercedes, Linea Vieja, Costa Rica. Period VI (800-1525 A.D.). Private collection, San José, Costa Rica.*

153 *Basalt table with openwork panels: crocodiles, birds and human figures. Height 67 cm. From Costa Rica. Period VI (800-1525 A.D.). Private collection, Panamá, Panamá.*

154 *Jadeite pendants. The largest is 14 cm. From Linea Vieja, Costa Rica. Period unknown. Private collection, San José, Costa Rica.*

155 *Jadeite pendants. Length 5 and 6 cm. From Linea Vieja, Costa Rica. Period unknown. Private collection, San José, Costa Rica.*

156 *Jadeite pendants representing birds. The largest is 4 cm. long. From Linea Vieja, Costa Rica. Period unknown. Private collection, San José, Costa Rica.*

157-158 *Jadeite mace-heads. The largest is 7 cm. in diameter. From Linea Vieja, Costa Rica. Private collection, San José, Costa Rica.*

159 *Gold pendant representing a frog. Length 8 cm. From Aguas Zarcas, San Carlos plain, Costa Rica. Period VI (800-1525 A.D.). Collection of Evelyn de Goicoechea, San José, Costa Rica.*

160 *Gold pendant representing a jaguar. Height 4.5 cm. From Aguas Zarcas, San Carlos plain, Costa Rica. Period VI (800-1525 A.D.). Collection of Evelyn de Goicoechea, San José, Costa Rica.*

(All the photographs were taken by Mr. Jack Birchall except Nos. 1 and 84 to 89, which were taken by the author.)

INDEX

Printed in Switzerland

THE TEXT AND ILLUSTRATIONS
IN THIS VOLUME WERE PRINTED
ON THE PRESSES OF NAGEL
PUBLISHERS IN GENEVA

FINISHED IN JUNE 1970
BINDING BY NAGEL PUBLISHERS,
GENEVA

PLATES ENGRAVED BY PHOTO-CHROMO-GRAVURE, LYONS

LEGAL DEPOSIT No 507

PRINTED IN SWITZERLAND

BRITISH
HONDURAS

Bay Islands

GUATEMALA

Naco

HONDURAS

Copán

Los Naranjos

MOSQUITIA

Comayagua

Lo de Vaca
Yarumela
Las Vegas

Tenampua

Chalchuapa

Tazumal
Cihuatan

San Salvador

EL SALVADOR

Los Llanitos

Choluteca

NICARAGUA

Gulf of
Fonseca

Lake Managua

CHONTALES

Managua

Lake
Nicaragua

Rivas
Ometepe Is.

SAN CARLOS

Papagayo

Bay of
Culebra

Bagaces

Tempisque
Valley CASTE

COSTA

Guapiles

GUANA
Nicoya

LINEA
VIEJA

PACIFIC

San José

CENTRAL
VALLEY

Las Huacas

Cartago

Limón

RICA

TALAMANCA

DIQUIS

OCEAN